FEARS, TEARS AND CHEERS!

THE ROLLER COASTER REHAB
OF A FEARFUL RESCUE DOG

By Lisa Benn

DEDICATION

Dedicated to all the incredible animals and humans that have taught me so much on my behaviour and healing journey.

To Forever Hounds Trust for their unwavering commitment to finding troubled hounds their forever homes; and finally, to the two main protagonists, Tam and Maia for the fun, laughter, Fears, Tears and Cheers!

With grateful thanks to Susan Kerry Bedell for her invaluable assistance in editing and formatting.

ISBN 978-1-913319-80-9

INDEX

INTRODUCTION - Just the two of us

For nearly five years it had been just me and Tam, my golden retriever. My huge, hairy, supremely cuddly, slobbery and dare I say it, slightly thuggish companion. Tam might be a bit of a lump and perhaps not the brightest spark, but he is one of the kindest dogs I have ever met. He is hugely sensitive with an innate ability to charm everyone he meets with his boundless enthusiasm for life and his heart of gold.

From eight weeks old Tam had been an only dog, rewarded with my undivided time and attention. For years we had taken long walks together, shared the sofa together and watched some pretty terrible TV together. We had faced life's challenges together, the highs, the lows, the ups, the downs yet all in all we had a lovely life.

Tam enjoyed a five star existence. He had a house full of toys, chews and bones. He feasted on top quality, grain free, hypoallergenic - hugely expensive - dog food with copious amounts of treats. He had a lovely garden to play in and never had to worry about sharing any-thing. What was mine was his, and if it wasn't he'd take it anyway!

Tam really was a great dog but when I think about it, it wasn't all plain sailing. There was the time when we were thrown out of puppy classes for being a disruptive influence on the other puppies. That wasn't a great day for a canine behaviourist! Then there was the time when I called Tam and he careered over to me at top speed, like a 36kg wrecking ball, and knocked me clean off my feet. It took me several minutes to regain my senses and get back on my feet and then another 15 minutes before the pain eased enough to take a step. Then then there were his allergies ... I won't go into detail but the sight that greeted me when I returned home from work one day was something to behold. So yes, we'd had the odd hiccup along the way but overall Tam was a pretty perfect dog.

I had made a lot of compromises to keep Tam happy and content. My previously pretty cottage garden with flowers thriving in the flower beds has been replaced with something that resembled the trench system in WW1. My beautiful well established shrubs succumbed to frequent golden showers, withered and died and my lovely green healthy lawn was reduced to a mud bath. My home suffered too. Gone were the clean carpets and furnishings, to be replaced with a patchwork of mis-matched rugs to protect what was left of the carpets, mud spatters on the walls, and my sofa hidden under so many throws I have forgotten what colour it is.

Then there was my social life which Tam obliterated. I felt so guilty leaving him home alone that I would turn down all social invitations. Instead, I would stay at home and play repetitive games like 'rolling the ball' which Tam always found fascinating and his favourite game, 'shred the cardboard' where his destructive tendencies were fully indulged. Yep, I was living the dream folks, living the dream!

There was just one thing that bothered me. Tam was such a friendly, sociable soul and I was increasingly aware that he was getting quite lonely whenever I went out. It didn't come as much of a surprise. Dogs have been bred for many generations to crave the company of humans, so it is understandable that many struggle to cope when we leave them home alone. Tam was always really friendly with other dogs. He enjoyed meeting his friends out on walks and loved mixing with friends' dogs whenever we went to visit. I started to consider how he would benefit from having a brother or sister to keep him company when I was not around. He would love a little friend, wouldn't he?

Just the two of us

ONE - The decision

The decision to take in a second dog was not taken lightly. Not only did I have to consider the impact on Tam's life, I also had to think long and hard about the effect it would have on my own. Dogs need so much time and I was busy with work and keeping Tam in the style to which he had become accustomed. Then there was the extra expense of taking on another dog. Another mouth to feed, routine veterinary care, insurance, toys, bedding, collar and lead, harnesses, coats, not to mention an almost limitless amount of treats. All in all, it would be a huge financial commitment for perhaps the next 15 years. I would only take in a second dog when I knew I had the time and finances to secure them a home, forever.

After several months and much deliberation I felt that the time was right to find Tam a friend. With so many thousands of dogs looking for homes it seemed a daunting task. Through my work, I saw on a near daily basis, the consequences of what happens when the 'wrong' dog ends up in the 'wrong' home and I was totally committed to making sure that I would avoid the pitfalls and find the 'right' dog for us. With so many things to consider, how would I find 'the one'?

I set about creating a wish list of all the essential criteria my new dog must fulfil. The first thing was whether to look for a male or female dog. Tam is an entire male so I didn't want to bring in another male dog that might make Tam feel he had to defend his 'top dog' position. I also didn't want an un-neutered bitch as I certainly didn't relish the idea of a house full of puppies a few months down the line. There are far too many unwanted dogs in the world as it is. I therefore decided that a neutered bitch would be the best fit.

Then I had to consider the age. Ideally I was looking for a young adult dog, between the ages of 3-5 years ish. Their juvenile years would be behind them, but there would still be many years ahead of them. I was looking for them to be able to grow old together.

By far the most important thing to consider was the personality and temperament of the dog to make sure it would be a good match for Tam. As Tam had been an only dog for his whole life, it was vital that I found a dog that would be happy for him to be top dog. It had to be a dog that would let Tam take the lead, one that wouldn't boss him around or challenge him over toys or food, a dog that would look up to Tam as if he were their big brother.

Tam is a laid back chap so it was also important to find a dog that matched his energy levels. They had to be playful but not boisterous, happy to have a mad five minutes with Tam but then able to settle and snooze. A high energy dog like a springer spaniel or a collie would be waaaay too much for him.

The dog would also have to fit in with my lifestyle. I have to go out to work, so I needed to find a dog that once it had settled in, would cope with being left at home with Tam for several hours a day without becoming stressed. So many dogs suffer from separation related issues which can have a hugely negative impact on their quality of life. Through my work I have seen some extreme cases, including a dog that was so distressed when it was left home alone it actually chewed its way through a solid wooden door to get out of the house. My new dog would have to be able to cope without me being around all day and be happy to have just Tam for company.

I also felt it was important that I take in a dog with some sort of behavioural problem that would make them otherwise difficult to rehome. No dogs are difficult for the sake of being difficult. There is always good reason behind the behaviour. Well, there's always a good reason from the dog's perspective, even if it's not immediately obvious to their human! I have spent a lifetime studying canine behaviour and have extensive experience working with 'difficult' dogs so it would be great to use these skills to help another dog in need. I am also a healing practitioner, specialising in animal healing and often use healing energy to help animal (and human) clients. It is so rewarding working with very troubled dogs, the ones with extreme fear, trust or anxiety issues. Healing can be incredibly powerful to help these dogs build trust and confidence and it is such a privilege to help them overcome their emotional traumas. It seemed a wasted opportunity if I didn't use my knowledge and skills to help a troubled dog.

There were a couple of exceptions. I couldn't take on a dog with any history of aggression because I had to protect Tam, and a dog with separation related problems would be difficult to manage with my lifestyle. I was willing to consider pretty much anything else.

The last and by far the least important thing on my wish list was what the dog looked like. Ideally I didn't want another large dog as I only live in a small cottage and Tam takes up a huge amount of floor - and sofa - space. I also didn't really want another super hairy dog. Like most self-respecting golden retrievers, Tam tends to throw himself into puddles, the larger and muddier the better. Think of a hippo in a wallow and you get the picture. The sight and smell of two big wet, muddy, hairy dogs after returning home from a winter walk was a little too much to bear. But really, as long as the personality was right, I wasn't bothered about the outer packaging.

After considering all options I knew what I was looking for. My new dog would be a spayed bitch, 3-5 years of age, low to medium energy, dog friendly, a follower rather than a leader and have some behaviour problems but not separation or aggression related. So, that was my wish list. Now all I had to do was find her.

TWO - The search begins

Once the decision had been made, I started to trawl through the websites of dog rescue charities. Heavens, where to start? There are literally thousands of rescue centres up and down the country, all full to bursting with lovely dogs all desperately waiting for their forever home.

First I went to the large national rescue centres, the RSPCA, Dogs Trust and the Blue Cross. I clicked onto their 'dogs seeking homes' pages and scrolled through thousands of photos of dogs. There were all shapes and sizes, all personalities and ages. I scanned through the photos and goodness that was sad. So many stressed, tense, confused faces looking back at me through the computer screen. Occasionally I clicked on the 'more information' link to find out more about them and read terribly sad stories. Many pulled at my heartstrings but I knew I hadn't found 'the one' yet.

I then started looking at smaller charities, the ones that sometimes fall in the shadow of the larger ones. The charities that don't have the money to run big TV advertising campaigns or national mail outs but do amazing work due almost entirely to the efforts of a mighty team of volunteers. It would be great if I could support one of them.

As I scrolled through my local charities I came across one that specialised in rehoming sighthounds. Sighthounds are breeds of dog such as greyhounds and whippets, that love to chase. Unlike other breeds they rely primarily on their excellent eyesight and incredible speed to hunt rather than their sense of smell. They are friendly, gentle, sensitive dogs and they make wonderful pets. Contrary to popular belief, these beautiful dogs are very low maintenance. Affectionately known as 30mph couch potatoes by anyone who has had the pleasure of owning a sighthound as a pet, these lovely dogs are by nature very lazy and require very little exercise. So long as they can stretch their extremely long legs daily, have a comfortable sofa to sleep on and a human slave to attend to their every whim, they are happy!

This got me thinking. I had owned a wonderful whippet crossbreed called Jas before I got Tam and she had been an incredible dog. Perhaps a sighthound would be a good fit for Tam and me. Lovely, gentle temperament, cheeky with a sense of humour, a bit on the tall side, but mainly all legs. Playful but lazy, not too boisterous - and an added bonus they are usually mud averse and have very short, odour -free, quick-drying hair.

I clicked onto this charity's website and started to scroll down the page looking at all their dogs that were available for rehoming. One photo caught my eye. It was of a lovely sweet fawn coloured little lurcher called Sunny who had become homeless through no fault of her own. She'd had a good start in life and had been a much loved family member until a change in her owners circumstances left her without a home. Her advert read that she was house-trained, sociable, friendly to other dogs, people and children; she walked nicely on a lead, could be left alone during the day, the positive points were endless.

What was clear was that she would be able to come home and fit in with family life almost immediately. Sounded perfect. There was just one thing that made me hesitate. Perhaps she was just a little *too* perfect. This was a lovely dog who I was sure would be very easy to rehome. She could fit in with most families, perhaps even a first time dog owner, and give them years of love and joy. I was in the position to offer a troubled dog a home, a dog that was difficult to rehome and one that would potentially spend years in kennels before facing an uncertain future. Whilst I felt I could offer Sunny a lovely home, it almost felt like I was being selfish. If I took her on, I would be depriving a less experienced family a wonderful dog and at the same time would be condemning a troubled dog to a life in kennels. I felt I needed to continue my search.

It was getting quite late and I had spent many hours looking through the pages of dozens of rescue centres. I had read profiles of hundreds of fabulous dogs but I knew deep in my heart that I still hadn't found 'the one'. I had a really strong feeling that she was out there patiently waiting, but after rejecting so many dogs I was starting to wonder if I would ever manage to find her.

For my final search that evening I went on to the Forever Hounds Trust Facebook page. Forever Hounds Trust works tirelessly to rescue, rehabilitate and home sighthounds and lurchers.

Many of the dogs they rescue are ex-racing greyhounds that are no longer considered of any use to the industry, either through injury or by not making the grade. I had put off looking at their page as they were not local to me, but as I hadn't found the right dog in the local rescue centres, I felt it was time to broaden my search area and give them a try. I scrolled down the page and looked at all the dogs that were available for rehoming and one strained little face instantly jumped out at me. It was my first glimpse of Maia. Oh wow, could she really be 'the one?'

Maia's Facebook advert read…

> "Sometimes we have a dog who needs a very special type of forever home. That's the case for little lurcher Maia. This beautiful girl is very shy, particularly fearful of men and can't live with a cat. But, she has a sweet and cheeky personality that starts to shine through when she feels safe.
>
> Could you offer her a patient and understanding forever home where she can take time to gain confidence and learn that life isn't all scary? Forever Hounds Trust will offer plenty of support throughout."

After reading Maia's advert I felt an immediate connection. It is hard to pinpoint exactly what called out to me, but I knew that Maia was destined to be my dog. I looked closely at her photos, trying to see beyond her tense boney body, past the dull, patchy 'kennel coat' and looked deeply into her huge, troubled eyes. It struck me how dark they were - almost black. It was like the 'windows to the soul' had been blacked out so no one could see in. I was completely overcome by a huge wave of emotion. I felt her sadness and pain, her confusion and despair. She was so lost and in such desperate need of a loving, understanding home. Oh my goodness, I knew that she was definitely meant to be my dog.

I decided to go on to the Forever Hounds Trust website to read Maia's online advert and see if I could find out any other scrap of information about her.

Maia's website advert read …

> "Beautiful, shy Maia is desperately looking for a new family, to teach her that people can be kind. Can you help?
>
> Maia is a young saluki/whippet cross who originally came to us from Ireland. We don't know much about her early life, but it is clear that poor Maia must have been treated very badly by humans in the past. She is painfully shy of new people, and especially fearful of men. Although Maia has been previously adopted, her nervousness causes her to struggle with home life. Unfortunately, she has recently found herself back in kennels for the third time because of this.

> *Maia is a fun-loving girl with a sweet, cheeky personality which starts to shine through when she feels safe. However, she needs a very special home in order to flourish and although she likes other dogs she DOES NOT get on with cats. Maia takes a lot of confidence from the company of other dogs, and will need to live with at least one other dog in her new home. Her ideal home would be one without any resident men, so that she can learn to trust men at her own pace. She has never shown any aggression, but so far has not been able to cope in a home with a resident man. Maia's new family will need to be very patient and understanding, as she will take a long time to settle in and feel comfortable around them. Less is definitely more with Maia, and she will gain confidence only if she is put under no pressure to interact with people. Experience with very nervous dogs would be helpful, but is not necessary as Maia's new family will have plenty of support and guidance from our behaviour team.*
>
> *Maia is such a sweet little girl, and a favourite with all our volunteers. She is only a baby, but has been through so much already and needs a kind, gentle family to show her that life isn't all scary! She just needs a quiet, low-pressure home environment with owners who will give her the space she needs to settle in. If you think you have the time and patience to give Maia the life she really does deserve, please get in touch".*

I was trying to be objective and think with my head and not my heart as re-read Maia's advert through increasingly blurred, teary eyes. I tried to weigh up all the pros and cons, but every time I looked into those dark, sad eyes, I felt an incredible emotional connection to her.

It was clear that I had two options. I re-read the advert for Sunny. She would be the easy option, a beautiful dog with no known issues. Then there was Maia. Maia was definitely a little more, how can I put this, 'complicated'. I would have to make huge changes to accommodate her and our lives would clearly never be the same again. It was a clear choice between easy street or a dog with very significant issues.

One main point kept coming to the fore and that was that beautiful Sunny would be easy to rehome. She would fit in with many families and had a really positive future. Maia's future looked a lot bleaker. On balance it was a no-brainer. It had to be Maia.

I read Maia's advert one more time before I typed the immortal words...

> *" I might be able to offer a suitable home to this beautiful girl. I have completed your online form and really look forward to hearing from you "*.

I took a deep breath and clicked 'send'. Now there was no going back!

After completing the online application form, I had an agonising wait for Forever Hounds Trust to get back to me. I was sure I could offer Maia her perfect home and help her overcome her trauma and give her the best opportunity to enjoy a really happy life. However, there were several stumbling blocks that I was worried might thwart my application. Firstly, I didn't have a solid six foot fence all around my garden. Lurchers are renowned for their ability to hurdle fences. I was prepared to re-fence my garden for Maia but would my word be enough of a guarantee? Secondly, Tam was an un-neutered male and it was Forever Hounds Trust policy that they don't home to families with un-neutered dogs and thirdly, my work takes me all across the south of England, so some days I am out of the house for more than their specified four hours a day. I prayed that the type of home I could offer and my experience would be enough for the charity to see beyond these, ahem, little issues and consider homing Maia with me.

I barely slept at all that night. There were a million questions running through my mind but frustratingly no answers. I was just going to have to be patient. That was a really long night!

Then the call came. I had a lovely long chat (or what could perhaps be better described as a thorough grilling!) with a wonderful lady called Katie from Forever Hounds Trust. I was questioned at length about my home, about Tam, my lifestyle and my work commitments. It was so reassuring to hear how much effort they made to ensure the right dog went to the right home. Then I had the opportunity to ask questions about Maia. I wanted to know *everything* about her, her history, personality and in particular the extent of her problems. Katie was incredibly patient and answered all my queries. We were on the phone for almost an hour, and despite the complications with my application, we made it past the first hurdle and my application would be considered. Phew. The next stage was to arrange to meet Maia.

Very little is known of Maia's life prior to arriving into the care of Forever Hounds Trust. She had been rescued in Ireland and then brought to England by the charity. By the time I spotted her advert on their Facebook page, she had been in the care of Forever Hounds Trust for EIGHTEEN MONTHS! It was hard to comprehend that a young dog could have spent such a terribly long time in kennels. She had been rehomed twice in that time but returned on both occasions due to fear-related behaviour issues. By the time I saw her advert, Maia had been back in kennels for five months and the charity was making one last attempt to find the perfect home for her. They had tried so hard with Maia but if she couldn't cope in kennels and she couldn't cope in a home, she was running out of options. I hoped with all my heart that my home was the one Maia had been waiting for.

Maia's website and Facebook advert photos

THREE - Our first meeting

After what seemed like an endless wait the day finally arrived when I would get to meet Maia for the first time. Forever Hounds Trust rescues and homes dogs from rented spaces at commercial boarding kennels. The kennels where Maia was being cared for was a couple of hours' drive from my home which gave me a lot of time to think. That's never a good thing for a behaviourist! I was trying to be philosophical: if she was the right dog to join our family, it would be obvious. I would get that feeling when I saw her and I would just *know*. Tam would have a lovely friend and life companion, someone with whom he could share his adventures and snuggle with when I wasn't home. I'd have another canine companion, another soul to love and care for and a furry friend to fill that spare seat on the sofa. It would all be wonderful. In my less philosophical moments my mind went into overdrive, running through all the things that could go wrong and thinking how this could all be a huge disaster. What if Tam and Maia hated each other? What if Maia hated me? What if I couldn't help her? This could all be a terrible decision that I could regret for the rest of my days. No pressure then!

As I got closer to the kennels, I took several unplanned detours courtesy of my satnav. Despite this, I made it a few minutes early which gave me a chance to calm myself down and get in the right headspace before meeting Maia.

I was greeted in the car park by Karen, the volunteer regional coordinator. After some niceties, we made our way through to the kennels. Oh my, this was it! The moment I had been waiting for. I was feeling such a mix of emotions. This meeting could change the whole focus of my life.

We passed through a narrow gateway and into a small feed room crammed full of 'stuff'. There were several big bins full of dog food. Assorted leads, harnesses and muzzles hung from hooks on the walls and there were piles of dog coats and clean bedding all neatly folded waiting to be distributed to the kennel residents. There was a notice board on the wall listing all the dogs currently in spaces, noting any special instructions or dietary requirements. It all seemed very orderly. We continued through a doorway and along a passageway. Kennels lined this passageway to our left, and to our right there was a grey tarpaulin hanging down to shield the dogs from the elements, which was gently flapping in the breeze.

The kennels were spotlessly clean but pretty basic. Each was painted

My first glimpse of Maia

Visit 2 - after healing

white, approximately four metres deep by two metres across, with bars floor to ceiling at the front. They were divided by breeze block walls with bars above that to the ceiling. Each kennel consisted of a run with a partially enclosed sleeping area at the back that afforded the residents a little privacy.

As we proceeded down the passageway, excited dogs rushed to the front of their kennels to greet us, all vying for our attention. Some barked, some jumped up and down, and some stood quietly wagging their tails appeasingly, hoping we would stop and talk to them. It was quite emotional. All these lovely friendly dogs were serving time through no fault of their own, just waiting until their human found them and took them to their forever home. I hoped with all my heart that one of the residents would soon be coming home with me.

We eventually came to a halt outside Maia's kennel. I was struck by how barren her kennel was. Just like all the others, it had a main run at the front, empty except for a clean blanket on the floor for Maia to lie on. The kennel had just been cleaned so the floor was wet. There was a food bowl which still contained some dry kibble left over from breakfast and a bowl on the floor contained clean fresh water. Maia's sleeping quarters at the back of the kennel contained a hard plastic dog bed with a nice soft vetbed and a clean folded blanket on the top for her to sleep on. Despite being basic, it looked comfortable and very clean. The only other item in the kennel was a rather tatty soft toy teddy lying on the floor in the corner. As I was taking everything in, I felt quite shocked. This small cell had been Maia's world for many months. When I considered all that Tam had, it was a real wake up call to see how this was the reality for thousands of dogs waiting to be homed in rescue centres up and down the country.

Then I got my first glimpse of Maia. Unlike the other dogs, she made no attempt to engage us. In fact the moment she saw us, she quickly retreated into her sleeping area at the back of her kennel. She went the furthest she could go to get away from us. It was devastatingly sad. In that moment I felt so much love for that little hound. I could feel how scared she was and sensed her panic when she realised we were stopping outside her kennel. What must she have gone through to make her this fearful of humans?

She was terrified. She hid in the corner of the kennel, pressing her little body into the cold breeze block wall in an attempt to appear invisible. Her posture was tense and her head held low. Her ears were pinned back, and there was fear in her huge dark eyes. As she stood willing us to leave, she was violently trembling from head to toe. She even urinated where she stood. I have to admit, no amount of warning had fully prepared me for this. The charity had done so much to help this little lurcher but it was clear that Maia wasn't coping in kennels and after two unsuccessful rehoming attempts, it seemed she couldn't cope in a home environment either.

I avoided looking at Maia and turned down the offer to enter her kennel. I so wanted to go in and give her a huge hug and tell her that she was safe and never had to fear anything ever again, that she had a lovely big brother waiting for her and a home full of toys, a sofa, yummy food and treats, but I knew that was the opposite to what Maia wanted. She just wanted us to leave her alone.

It was vital in this first visit that I lay positive foundations for our future relationship. I had to show Maia that I would not ask any-thing of her or do anything to her without her consent. She was safe with me. I sat quietly on the wet floor outside her kennel. Without looking at her or talking to her I just sat and sent her some healing. One of the many benefits of healing is that it can be sent without having to make direct physical contact. This is invaluable when working with really fearful dogs like Maia. Animals are usually extremely sensitive to this energy and Maia was no exception. I sent very calming energy to her from outside of her kennel and I could see that she responded to it almost immediately.

It was freezing cold in that passageway and I had lost all feeling in my hands and feet but I knew Maia wasn't ready for me to enter her kennel. After about an hour, I looked at her through the corner of my eye. She had stopped trembling but she was still hiding at the back of her kennel looking anxious. Our peace was interrupted when it was suggested that I might like to see her outside on a walk. I made the, in hindsight pretty naïve, assumption that Maia would enjoy going for a walk so I agreed. I should have known better.

A harness, lead and coat were brought to Maia's kennel by one of the kennel staff. Instead of getting excited at the sight of the harness and prospect of going for a walk, Maia froze. As she was gently 'tacked up' in the harness, she stood trembling, silently crying out with every ounce of her being that she just wanted to be left alone. I felt terrible for her. She jumped when she was touched yet she made no attempt to flee, she just stood motionless with her tail clamped so far between her legs it was almost touching her belly. She was in a 'learned helplessness' state, a behaviour observed when dogs know they have no opportunity to avoid unpleasant situations and have no control over what will happen to them.

Instead of fighting, Maia shut down, put up no resistance and waited for it all to come to an end. It broke my heart seeing her so scared in a scenario that was meant to be fun!

As the kennel door opened I stood as far back as I could to avoid adding to Maia's stress. As soon as she exited the kennel she towed the handler down the passageway and out of the kennel block. She seemed very uneasy walking past the other dogs and was clearly trying to get from A to B as quickly as possible.

Outside the kennel block was a small paddock that contained pens where the dogs could get out of their kennels and get some fresh air. The pens were each approximately three metre squares of grass enclosed by three metre high metal fencing. Each contained one dog. We started to walk round the edge of the paddock but Maia looked so scared that there seemed little point continuing. She was taken into an empty pen and her lead was unclipped so she could have some time to herself. As she walked round the pen she started to take an interest in her surroundings. She sniffed the grass and glanced up at the dogs in the other pens. Although she was still very much on edge, it was good to see her start to let her defences down.

We gave Maia plenty of time to settle in the pen on her own before I joined her. As soon as I entered, she immediately moved to the far side of the pen. It was clear that she was anticipating that I would try and approach her so I did the opposite and walked away. I stood at the far side of the pen with my back to her, adopting a soft posture to make myself appear non-threatening. I wanted to sit on the ground but luckily I was reminded that Maia wasn't the first dog to use that pen that day!

Once Maia understood that I wasn't going to try and do anything to her, she went back to sniffing the grass. It was a great sign that she was starting to accept my presence. In order to confirm that I wasn't a threat to her, I walked away from her. That got her attention. She stopped sniffing and watched me intently. I could feel her staring at me, poised to run if necessary but also daring herself to trust me. Great! Now I had sparked her interest I could work with her. Even though I hadn't said anything to Maia or even looked at her, lines of communication were open.

I walked back to the other side of the pen, not looking at her and keeping as far away from her as I could. I could see in the corner of my eye that she had taken a couple of steps towards me. Result! That was my cue to walk away from her again. I repeated this several times. Each time Maia grew a little in confidence until she was warily following me around the pen. To me, this was a huge breakthrough. It confirmed that I could help her. I was sure that Maia wanted to get to know me but she was so fearful of people that she didn't quite dare.

As we hung out in the pen another resident, a golden retriever, walked past us on his way back to his kennel. When Maia saw him her energy changed. Her tail went up and she trotted towards him. It was great to see her looking animated. It was also a relief to see in that fleeting moment that Maia liked golden retrievers!

When it was time for Maia to return to her kennel, she started to walk back but then it all became too much for her and she planted her feet and froze. Her handler gently picked her up and carried her back to her kennel. My heart broke for this sad, lost little hound.

I waited for Maia to be untacked then I joined her in her kennel. I sat on the floor just inside the door and again avoided making any eye contact or interacting with her. Maia lay in her bed and watched me as I quietly sent her healing. But this time something was different. She had stopped trembling and was watching me curiously. Instead of willing me to go away, she was slightly less defensive and perhaps even dare I say, a little more open to learning about me. This was a huge shift for such a fearful and shut down dog. The changes were subtle but they were there. How I wanted to approach her and give her a hug, but I knew that would compromise all the trust that had started to build. Instead I just quietly left her kennel and closed the door behind me.

Just before I left, I turned and looked at Maia. She was watching me with a quizzical look on her face. I had spent just over two hours with her yet I had not tried any funny business. I had not approached her, touched her, or done anything to her. This was unusual behaviour from a human! Instead I had just sent her healing which had been comforting and relaxing. Perhaps I wasn't like all the others? Then for the first time, I made eye contact with Maia. Wow, it was such a profound moment, one I will never forget. As I looked into her eyes, she looked back at me and stared deeply into my eyes. It is almost impossible to describe that moment except to say it was a meeting of souls. A deep, deep knowing that we had found each other.

Now there was no going back.

FOUR ~ Our second meeting

It was a very long week before I was able to visit Maia again. I tried not to get too excited or have too many expectations about our next meeting but it was impossible. She had been in my thoughts almost constantly since our first visit.

I pulled up into the kennels. Would I feel the same when I saw Maia again? Would she remember me from our last visit and how would she react? I was quite nervous as I approached her kennel. When she saw us approach she immediately ran to the back of her kennel. This time I went straight in and without looking at her or trying to engage her in any way, I sat on the floor at the front of the kennel. I sat as far away as I could to give her as much space as possible but it was still too close for Maia to feel comfortable. She lay in her bed and trembled, her worried eyes looking in vain for some way of escape. It was heart-breaking. As before, I completely ignored her. I knew that if I just sat quietly and sent Maia healing again, she would begin to relax.

After about 20 minutes I noticed that she had stopped trembling. This was a great sign as it showed her stress levels were starting to go down. I continued to send her healing for a further 40 minutes and then started to notice the expression on her face changing. There was less tension in her jaw and face and her eyes seemed slightly softer. There was no doubting the connection between us. I felt that Maia would be able to cope with me if I edged slightly closer. As I shuffled along a few inches I could see her anxiety levels leap up again but she didn't show the extreme fear as when I entered her kennel. I sat quietly and waited for her to settle again. I had been told by Forever Hounds Trust that Maia was rather partial to chicken so I had come prepared and brought a huge bag of diced roasted chicken with me. From my slightly closer vantage point I rolled a little piece towards Maia. My aim wasn't great and it fell short of my target but it got her attention. I rolled another piece that landed just in front of her. From the corner of my eye I could see her nose frantically twitching. Would she be brave enough - or greedy enough - to take it? It didn't take long. After a short time she reached forward with her long pointy nose and delicately took the chicken. She put it down on the floor in front of her and inspected it. Well you can't be too careful can you! After a short deliberation she decided it was safe to proceed and ate it.

I stayed in Maia's kennel for about another hour. Sitting quietly, sending healing and rolling pieces of chicken in her direction. To an observer it probably looked about as exciting as watching paint dry but I knew we were making really important progress. This was the foundation onto which I would build our relationship. Laying foundations takes time and patience. I knew it would pay dividends down the line.

I had been sitting in Maia's kennel for two hours yet it only felt like 20 minutes. I wanted to stay longer so that Maia could learn as much about me as possible but our visit had to come to an end. I could feel all my love pouring out of my heart to hers and I desperately wanted to take her home there and then. However we still had one final hurdle to negotiate. A big hairy golden one…!

FIVE ~ Tam and Maia's first meeting

After two visits I had fallen hook, line and sinker for Maia, but I can't say that the feeling was entirely mutual. We had spent four hours together yet I still hadn't touched her or talked to her - I had barely even looked at her - but in the time we spent together there was something more meaningful going on. I was sure I could offer her a home that would allow her to heal from her past traumas and become the dog she was always meant to be. But more than that, I felt a profoundly deep connection; she was destined to be with me.

I was all ready to bundle her into my car and take her home at the first opportunity but I still had to get Tam's approval. How would he take to Maia? How would she respond to him? Could she really be the companion that I had hoped and dreamed I would find for Tam? There was only one way to find out. It was time for them to meet.

After discussion with the Forever Hounds Trust team, we agreed on a quiet location. It was a lovely secure dog walking field just a short drive from kennels, which gave the hounds in the charity's care the chance to have a good run and get away from the stresses of kennel life. The field is owned by one of the fabulous charity volunteers, Tammy who regularly visited Maia in kennels to give her companion-ship, not to mention stuffed Kongs and home-cooked chicken, and was introduced to me as 'Maia's favourite person'.

The date was set for Tam and Maia to meet the following week. I have to admit I got very little sleep that week and my emotions were in tatters. I tried to take the fatalistic 'what will be, will be' attitude and not to get too excited but my mind knew better! It was racing with conflicting thoughts and emotions. Every time I closed my eyes I could see those big dark haunted eyes staring back at me, deep, deep into my eyes. My heart yearned for her but the decision was not mine to make. The final decision had to be Tam's.

During that never-ending week, I planned everything to the enth degree. I considered every possible scenario for how to introduce Tam and Maia and I have quite some imagination! What if Tam didn't like Maia? What if Maia didn't like Tam? What if Maia ran away and couldn't be caught? I had reoccurring visions of Maia racing around the field in a mad panic trying to evade capture. Urgh, my mind was really spinning. Funnily enough I didn't give much consideration to the possibility that all might actually go smoothly! My philosophy is to prepare for the worst so you are ready for every eventuality and anything better is a pleasant surprise.

The day finally arrived! We couldn't have wished for a more beautiful day. It was late spring, the sun was shining, the sky was clear and there was a gentle breeze, perfect to keep the dogs cool. There was so much riding on this introduction and it was vital we got it right. If things didn't go well, I would have regrets for the rest of my days. If it did go well, all of our lives would change forever.

Tam does not travel well, so I picked up some medication from my vet to help him on the long journey to Bedfordshire. We arrived at the agreed location. It was a beautiful home in a tranquil setting, very secluded. It was perfect for Tam and Maia's first meeting.

My first concern was to get Tam to the paddock to have a good sniff and have a bit of a run so he would be nice and calm when he met Maia. Unfortunately Karen had the same idea and had also arrived early to allow Maia a chance to investigate the field before meeting Tam. Tam and I started walking towards the field across a beautifully manicured lawn and over a pretty little wooden bridge. I was so keen for Tam to make a good first impression. I wanted to show that I was a competent and responsible dog owner worthy of rehoming Maia, and that Tam would make a great big brother. Tam had other ideas. Having been cooped up in the car for more than two hours, he was ready for a run and he towed me all the way to the field! Oh dear, I tried to hide the fact that I was wrestling Tam with all my strength to try and keep him walking nice and steadily on the lead but it was obvious who was in control. Not the best start.

I opened the gate and took Tam into the paddock. I could see Maia standing with Tammy waiting patiently in the glorious sunshine. It was so wonderful to see her away from the noisy and oppressive kennel environment. Hopefully here Maia would be able to escape the stresses of her everyday life, start to relax and perhaps enjoy herself. I felt a huge outpouring of emotion when I saw her. So much rested on the next couple of hours. The stakes couldn't be higher.

Maia got worried as we entered the paddock. She stood with her tail clamped right down between her legs, her ears went flat back against her head and she watched us nervously. She looked so fragile and vulnerable. I really wanted to rush over and reassure her but I knew I had to keep my distance. Our time would come. It had been several months since Maia paid her last visit to the paddock so we were not sure how she would react. As it turned out, she was very happy to be back and stood sniffing the air and taking in the scenery. It almost seemed a shame that I had sabotaged her day out by arranging for my big hairy boy to come and join her!

As I walked round the paddock Tam was beyond excited. He was pulling on his lead, zig-zagging left and right sniffing at all the new, unfamiliar smells. He desperately wanted to go and explore so I took him to the far end of the paddock, away from Maia, and let him off the lead. After having a good whizz round, Tam got down to business, trotting round to familiarise himself with his surroundings. He seemed completely oblivious to Tammy and Maia so I gradually took him a little further up the paddock to be a little closer to them.

One of the scenarios that I agonised over during my sleepless nights was that Tam would be too bullish around Maia. Whilst he is quite confident, super friendly and signals really well to other dogs, I was concerned his exuberance might make him a bit overwhelming and intimidating for her. I need not have worried, to my surprise he was far more interested in leaving his mark on the paddock for future dogs to read rather than saying hello to Maia. He actually seemed quite disinterested in her. This was good news for an initial first meeting but I have to admit that a little part of me had hoped that they would hit it off straight away and it would be love at first sight.

After Tam had explored the paddock, I put him back on the lead for a formal introduction. By this time Maia had had quite a lot of time to watch us from a distance. She had observed Tam's behaviour and got a sense of his energy without being under any pressure and I hoped she was starting to realise that despite his slightly bullish demeanour Tam was actually a really nice chap.

I was mindful that Maia would not just have the stress of meeting Tam, but she would also have to cope with me approaching her too at the other end of Tam's lead. We walked up to her calmly from the side to ensure good, polite dog etiquette was observed. If given the choice, dogs rarely greet other dogs head-on as it can be quite confrontational, so approaching at an angle is always best. I tried to keep my distance as much as possible and let Tam introduce himself. Maia was quite unsure and moved away. I think it's fair to say that she wasn't exactly thrilled to meet us! Despite Tam's polite greeting Maia made it perfectly clear that she really wasn't at all interested in making further acquaintance with him. I think she was pretty over-whelmed by his friendly, but slightly full-on greeting along with my presence a couple of metres away. After the briefest of acknowledg-ments, that was it. It was all a bit of an anti-climax.

I decided to let Tam off the lead again so he could he could continue his exploration of the field. I was a little concerned that he might run over to Maia in a boisterous, golden retriever, kind of way but he was far too busy. With nose down and tail up, he trotted around the paddock familiarising himself with every tiny smell. This was good and bad. While I didn't want him to run up to Maia, I had hoped that he would show a bit more interested in her. It certainly wasn't the love at first sight scenario. It was more of a shrug of the shoulders and underwhelming indifference.

It was such a beautiful day, I sat on the grass with Tammy and Karen and we chatted about Maia and the amazing work Forever Hounds Trust was doing. As we were talking, Maia let her guard down, found an acceptable spot and lay flat out on the grass catching some rays. It was such a wonderful sight. After the stress of living in kennels she was finally enjoying some peace.

While she was sleeping, I had my first opportunity to have my first proper look at her. She painted such a sad picture. The charity does everything possible to ensure the health and happiness of all the hounds in their care but the reality is that some dogs cope better in kennels than others. It seemed to me that kennel life had taken its toll on Maia. Her coat was patchy and dull and the hair on her temples had thinned revealing her grey skin beneath. I was also struck by the lack of muscle definition on her back, quarters, shoulders and thighs from months of restricted lead walk exercise. She was an acceptable weight for her size and breed, but her tense posture and extensive muscle wastage defined several vertebrae on her back. Maia also had old scars on her face, legs and abdomen that one could only speculate what she went through to get them. The last thing that struck me was how bony her tail was. It has to be said that Tam has a splendidly bushy tail. Maia had the skinniest tail I had ever seen on a dog of her size. It was so skinny that you could clearly see every bone in her tail. It was a bit freaky!

Eventually and somewhat reluctantly, we had to think about bringing our meeting to an end. It had been the most wonderful day. The dogs seemed so settled by this time, quietly lying on the grass next to us, it seemed a shame to disturb them but there was still something we needed to do. After brief discussion we all agreed that we should let Maia off the lead and let her have her first off lead run for many months. As Tammy unclipped her, we watched with bated breath as Maia cantered over to the fence and started to sniff the grass. This caught Tam's attention and he trotted over to her. Perhaps she might be fun after all because she had been pretty boring up till now!

As Tam approached, Maia saw him and trotted off in the opposite direction. Tam wasn't going to be deterred by this brush-off and took off after her. When she realised she was being followed, Maia took fright. Her head went up, her tail clamped down and she broke into a canter in an attempt to get away from him. Tam seemed confused by her reaction. He had approached her in the spirit of friendship but he had been completely shunned.

I called him to me so we could give Maia some space. After a few minutes Tam decided to have another go at making friends. This time he approached a little more cautiously. He was very respectful of her space and was clearly making a concerted effort not to get so close. This seemed more acceptable to Maia and she continued to sniff round the paddock with Tam following at an acceptable distance. When Maia stopped, Tam stopped and when she set off again so did he. He showed so much restraint, he really wanted to get to know Maia but was respectful of her need for space. This was such a great sign. Despite my reoccurring nightmare, we caught the dogs without any problems and our meetup ended on an optimistic note. There was just one thing left to do. I still had to ask Karen if she was happy for me to take Maia on and give her a forever home.

It had been such a great day and things had gone pretty well. Yes, it would have been wonderful if Tam and Maia hit it off immediately but there was no animosity between them and I felt confident that with time they would be able to work things out. I crossed my fingers as I asked the question and to my great relief, Karen looked delighted and just a little bit relieved. It turned out that my anxiety about whether Karen would allow me the privilege of rehoming Maia was matched by Karen's anxiety about whether I still wanted to have her. To our mutual delight, the decision was made. Cue tears all round! Maia would be coming home in seven days' time. I was absolutely thrilled.

We all made our way back to the parked cars. We offered the dogs a drink and I watched as Maia was lifted into the back of Karen's car. The next time I would see her would be when she came home. Forever. The decision had been made. Let the preparations begin!

Maia meets Tam

SIX - Let the preparations begin

I decided that in order to give Maia the best chance of settling in, I had to clear my diary for the next four weeks. It was difficult to know exactly how she would cope being in a home environment. There was little information about her life prior to being rescued by Forever Hounds Trust. Had she ever lived happily in a family home? She had been rehomed twice so I knew that she had spent a couple of short spells in a home environment but there were significant fear-related issues in both, hence her being returned. Her intense fear of humans certainly suggested that she had experienced significant abuse at some stage. I would have to slowly piece together what had happened in her past based on her reaction to all the new things she would encounter. I would prepare for her arrival as much as I could, but I would have to be ready to go to plan B or C - or perhaps plan J or K, or Q or R! The effects of spending such a long time in kennels must have had an impact on Maia's physical, mental and emotional health that could make it hard for her to settle into a home. The daily routine that she had followed for so long in kennels would be turned on its head. She was used to a simple existence with little stimulation and few changes. When she came home she would be confronted with countless unfamiliar noises, sights and smells. Everyday items that we take for granted like the vacuum cleaner, could overwhelm Maia after kennel life. After living on her own in her own kennel with only herself to worry about, she would have to get used to living with a new mum and a new big brother. She would have to share her space, learn to accept our behaviour and adjust to our routine. It was going to be a massive change for her.

I always feel a huge amount of empathy for animals that are sold or change hands, as they are so totally helpless in the decisions that define their future. They do not choose where they go or who they end up with, what they will eat or what routine they will follow. They don't even know if they will be treated kindly and respectfully or face abuse or neglect. We make those decisions for them. It must be such a scary time for any animal that gets rehomed and it is so easy to underestimate the challenge they face when settling into a new home. It is hard enough for confident animals that have enjoyed a happy life but for fearful animals like Maia, it must be terrifying.

It can also be easy to overlook the impact on the resident dog when introducing a new dog into the home. Tam had been an only dog for many years. He had got into a routine where he could do pretty much what he wanted when he wanted, so long as it was in accordance with house rules. When Maia arrived he would have to learn how to share everything. The exclusivity he had enjoyed for five years was about to change radically and I was concerned he would find it hard to adjust. Having a new little sister would be quite a challenge. I had to do all I could to prepare him for our new arrival and support him as she settled in.

I called all my Clients who had already booked appointments for the next few weeks to see if we could reschedule them. After extensive juggling of diaries, I managed to slot everyone in before my time off. It was going to be a busy week!

Next I had the fun job of going online and ordering Maia's tack and wardrobe. I had a lot of kit from my work, but this was a chance for some guilt-free dog shopping. Shopping for new dog essentials gives you all the fun of shopping without that little voice in the back of your mind saying "are you sure you really need that?" Yes, I could shop with a clear conscience. Spend, spend, SPEND!

I wrote out a considerable list of all the things Maia would need. First of all, a comfortable harness for when she was ready to go out for walks. As she was so scared of everything I would need one that was almost impossible for her to get out of if she took fright and panicked. The last thing I wanted was to watch Maia disappearing over the horizon whilst I was left holding a lead and empty harness! I decided on the 'Perfect Fit Harness' as they are very comfortable and can be adjusted to ensure a great fit and most dogs can't get out of them.

I also needed a double ended lead. These are leads that have a clip at each end so they can be attached to both a harness and a collar at the same time. This would give me a bit of a safety net so that if Maia slipped her collar, she would still be attached to me via her harness, or vice versa. One of my biggest fears was that I would be writing one of those 'Lost dog' ads on Facebook. I knew that if Maia were to get away from me I might never find her again and that didn't bear thinking about. As Tam has a black lead, I decided on a red lead for Maia. That way it would be much easier to see which lead belonged to which dog when I was out walking them together. If I needed to shorten Maia's lead quickly, I wouldn't have to waste valuable time working out which lead to grab.

I would need to make a few alterations to the layout of my home to accommodate Maia's needs. I felt it was really important to make these changes as soon as possible so that Tam had a chance to get used to them before Maia arrived.

In order for her to feel safe, I cordoned a little area in the corner of the living room beside the sofa exclusively for Maia. Dogs often feel safer if they have a small den-like area to retreat to. This would be Maia's go-to place if ever she felt worried, where she could be sure that she wouldn't be approached or disturbed by Tam or me. I put a dog mattress on the floor with a vetbed and a folded double duvet on the top for Maia to snuggle into. It looked so cosy I was tempted to sleep there myself! The final addition to her den would be an Adaptil plug-in diffuser. Adaptil is an artificial pheromone for dogs. Whilst it is odourless and undetectable to humans, it has been developed to send comforting messages to dogs to help them feel calm in stressful situations. I hoped this would help Maia feel a little more secure and help her settle in a little easier. I also hoped it might help Tam cope with the upheaval that was about to befall him.

My next job was to create a nice sleeping area for Maia upstairs. After much furniture shifting, the only practical place for a second dog bed would be on the floor next to my bed. For five years Tam had chosen to sleep at the foot of my bed, but I was concerned that when he saw Maia lying in the new bed right next to me, he might feel a bit put out. In order to give him a chance to choose where he wanted to sleep, I set up the second bed a few days before Maia was due to arrive. If Tam preferred sleeping there, I would make that Tam's bed and Maia could sleep in Tam's space at the foot of my bed. But Tam is a creature of habit. He slept in the new bed for the first night but then reverted back to his old bed. Decision made!

My list continued: food bowl, house collar, a dog tag engraved with contact details, toys. I wasn't sure what toys Maia would like. There was a small, well nibbled teddy in her kennel but that was her only toy. Tam had a *huge* selection of toys, many of which he hadn't played with for some time. I decided that I would let Maia choose toys from Tam's rejects. If I got new toys for Maia, Tam would want to play with them and I didn't want to create a situation where they might argue or build resentment over toys.

I contacted Forever Hounds Trust to find out what food Maia was eating at kennels and ordered a large bag in for her. She was going to encounter so much novelty, keeping to the same food would be something familiar and might help prevent an upset tummy. This can be very common problem when dogs move in to a new home due to a combination of stress and unfamiliar diet. Hopefully I could minimise the risk, especially considering that Maia might not be fully toilet trained! An added bonus was that the food she had been eating in kennels, whilst a good quality food, was much cheaper than Tam's special hypo-allergenic, grain-free food that cost well over £55 a bag.

My next job was to lurcher-proof my garden. Whilst it was secure for a 36kg golden retriever, ensuring it was safe for a lurcher would take some work. In order to comply with Forever Hounds Trust guidelines, I had to increase the fence height so that it was 6ft high to prevent Maia from jumping out. I also had to check the bottom of the fence to make sure that there were no holes she might be able to escape through. A gap impenetrable for Tam might not be such a challenge for a skinny little lurcher. It was quite a job but I was ably assisted by my wonderful neighbour and by the end of the day, my garden closely resembled Fort Knox. Get out of that one, Maia!

Then it was time to attack my home. My cottage was bearing the scars of having come out of a long winter with my golden retriever mud monster. If Forever Hounds Trust saw the state it was in, there was every chance that they would put Maia back in the car and take her straight back to Bedfordshire! It would take a super-human effort to get it ready for the scrutinising eyes of the charity, but Maia was worth it. I went to Waitrose and cleared their shelves of cleaning products. Let battle commence.

After considerable effort, my cottage started to look respectable. All I had to do was keep it that way! Finally, I asked Karen if she could bring some of Maia's bedding from the kennels with her. Dogs have an amazing sense of smell. It's waaay better than humans and it is really important to help them learn about their environment. I felt it could help Maia to settle in and feel safer if she had some familiar smells around her when she arrived. Hopefully her bedding and her little teddy would give her some comfort.

So, everything was ready. I was satisfied that I had done all that I could to prepare for Maia's arrival. All that was left now was to wait. I spent the evening with Tam making the most of our last few hours together, just the two of us. He knew that something was afoot but was blissfully ignorant about the enormity of what was about to hit him. Oh goodness, what have I done...?!

SEVEN ~ Maia comes home

Finally the day had arrived. After a restless night I woke bright and early. I tried so hard to contain my excitement and act like it was just a normal day but there was no fooling Tam. From the moment I woke, he knew something was up. He was really hyper. He kept grabbing his soft toys for comfort then running up to me and sitting in front of me, blocking my way, wanting attention and reassurance.

I decided to take him out for an early walk, hoping that he would then be nice and calm for when our visitors arrived. It would also allow enough time for him to dry out if he decided to take a dip in the river. A wet dog - or to put it more specifically that wet dog *smell* - wouldn't make a terribly good first impression of my home.

Our walk was uneventful but quite poignant as it marked the end of an era. For years we had walked up on the beautiful open downland that surrounds my cottage. It is so beautiful and peaceful up there and we rarely saw a soul. It would be some time before we would be able to venture up onto the hills again following Maia's arrival.

Back home and back to reality. There was just enough time for a quick run round with the vacuum cleaner and a last minute tidy. One last read through my check list and then all we could do was wait.

Tammy and Karen had kindly offered to bring Maia home, which spared Tam and me another four hour round trip. It would also be more comfortable for Maia as Karen's car is quite a lot bigger than mine. Karen was also bringing her lovely rescue greyhound Kora along for the ride to give Maia some company and some confidence. It was certainly going to be snug in my little old cottage!

Eventually, the car pulled up outside. I was soooo excited but also apprehensive. I watched anxiously through the window as it reversed on the drive. Tam had also seen the car and he could barely contain himself. He ran round the living room like a lunatic, grabbing at all the soft toys he could until he had three in his jowly chops!

I felt it would be easier for Maia if I waited in the cottage. She would be so scared and disorientated after her long journey, the last thing she needed was another scary human as soon as she got out of the car. Tammy gently lifted her out of the car. Maia was so scared she immediately urinated on the drive. Oh goodness my heart was in knots, poor Maia. It certainly gave us a clear indicator of how she was feeling and confirmed just how difficult this was for her.

As my guests approached the front door there was a brief moment of stillness and reflection and then chaos broke out! As soon as I opened the door, Tam turned into a whirling torpedo. He frantically grabbed at his soft toys before going into hospitality overdrive. He quickly rushed up to Tammy and Karen to welcome them before showing Kora around the rest of the cottage. He then rushed into the garden with an equally excited Kora in hot pursuit. It wasn't long before he came hurtling back in to say 'hello' again!

For Maia, it was rather less exciting. As she came into the cottage it was clear that she was completely overwhelmed. She trembled from head to toe and really didn't know what to do with herself. Where to run? Where to hide? Her posture was tense, her head held low and her tail clamped firmly between her legs. Every muscle in her body was tight. Her eyes were as wide as saucers, darting from left to right and her ears pinned back against the sides of her head. There was so much tension in her face and jaw and I could see her teeth firmly clenched. Poor girl, she was absolutely terrified.

I immediately showed Maia to her den so she knew where to go to feel safe. She went straight to the back and lay down, pressing into the wall. It reminded me of our first meeting in kennels a few weeks earlier. At least in her den she was safe and we could leave her there to acclimatise and get her bearings. Karen had brought some of Maia's old bedding with her so we put it next to her in the den along with her little nibbled teddy. Although they were a bit stinky, they were familiar to Maia and should bring her some comfort.

Although it might seem odd, I made the conscious decision not to interact with Maia while Tammy, Karen and Kora were there. She was so scared and disorientated, I knew that any interaction with me at that time would not be seen as a positive experience. There was no hurry. I would start to build our relationship once everyone had left and after Maia had plenty of time to settle.

After we had eaten lunch, we briefly took Maia out into the garden. It was such a beautiful day but Maia was far too scared to notice. She stood as she had done in the cottage, almost frozen in fear. She made no attempt to look around at all. She just wanted to return to the relative safety of the cottage.

We took a few photos for posterity and then returned inside. Maia jumped straight up on to the sofa. She certainly didn't waste any time in securing the most comfortable spot in the cottage! I left her harness on with a house line attached just in case I needed to get hold of her in an emergency but from here on in, Maia would be in the driving seat. All that was left to do was to complete the adoption paperwork for Forever Hounds Trust. Karen talked me through Maia's re-homing and insurance documents and gave me a tag with their contact details to attach to Maia's collar. Then that was it! Maia's new life with Tam and me had officially begun.

As we all got up, Maia jumped off the sofa and returned to her den. Tammy and Karen said their goodbyes and set off on their long journey home. They had been so incredibly kind and generous with their time. They were clearly very fond of Maia and so committed to finding a home where she could be safe and happy. I really hoped that my cottage would be that home. One thing was really odd. When Karen and Tammy went to leave, Maia stayed in her den and made no attempt to go with them. It was almost as if she knew that she was already home.

Then, it was just the three of us. After all the hustle and bustle, the cottage suddenly seemed very still and quiet. All those weeks of preparation, the sleepless nights, agonising over the best way forward had led to this moment. It seemed hard to comprehend that this sad, shut down, troubled little soul had actually come home and was now lying in her den trying to make sense of every-thing. But two had become three. After all the uncertainty in her life I was expecting this lost hound to take a huge leap of faith and trust me to take care of her. She had lived in so many different homes in her short life, how could I help her understand that this would be her last? It was my responsibility to do all that I could to help these two dogs live their best life. If that meant making huge financial and social sacrifices and spending the next ten years sitting on the floor whilst they snuggled up on the sofa, then so be it.

I left Maia in her den and made no attempt to approach or talk to her. She needed peace, time and space to learn about her new home with as little pressure as possible. I didn't know what specific things she was afraid of at this stage so I gave her a wide berth and tried to keep my movements a little slower and more deliberate than usual.

As I tidied up after my visitors, I did so as quietly as possible so that I didn't scare Maia, but I was very aware that she was watching my every move *very* closely. I had been so consistent in my behaviour during all our interactions I was confident that we would be start-ing on a positive footing now she had come home. Maia knew that I

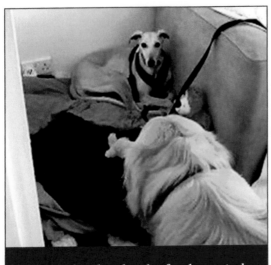

Maia in her den shortly after her arrival

First time in the garden

was quiet, calm and non-confrontational. I hadn't tried to make her do anything and when she felt uncomfortable I had listened and given her more space. I hadn't even made any attempt to touch her. All in all it was very strange behaviour for a human but I hoped that it was enough to have made my position clear.

Tam was visibly quite confused by Maia's behaviour. He kept walking up to her quietly, sniffed her nose then walked away with his tail wagging gently. It was like he was reassuring her but knew that she needed space. It was very unusual for him to react in this way as he is usually very excited to see other dogs. He would normally take his toys to them and encourage play. With Maia, he *knew* something was different. He had stepped into 'big brother' mode almost immediately. It was the best possible response.

As he was at a bit of a loose end, I called him over and gave him loads of praise. I wasn't going to make the mistake of giving Maia all my attention and leave Tam to feel side-lined. I needed Tam to know from the start that Maia was a positive addition to our lives. It was so important that he accepted her. We sat on the sofa and I quietly sent Maia and Tam some healing. Tam felt the energy immediately and settled next to me. I knew that by sharing this, Tam and Maia would be starting to form a lovely, pure, profound connection. I couldn't see Maia from where I was sitting but I knew she was picking up on the healing energy too. She had received a lot when I visited her in kennels and I had also sent her distant healing between visits. I was confident that she would find this comforting and reassuring. The cottage started to feel really calm and peaceful. It was as if everything else faded away and all that was left were three souls starting to connect. We stayed in the stillness for some time, taking in the energy and enjoying the peace. There was no better way to welcome Maia to our home and introduce her to Tam.

After about half an hour or so, something wonderful happened. I saw Maia's nose poking out from her den. It was only fleeting, but I definitely saw it! It was beyond even my most optimistic dreams. Maia was already tentatively starting to send out feelers and learn about her new home. Dogs that are extremely fearful can take many months or even years to recover from their trauma and some never fully recover from their physical or emotional scars. Maia would have all the time she needed for her recovery and I was completely committed to doing everything in my power to help her. By this stage I hadn't even touched Maia. The closest I had come to physical contact was when I briefly held her lead in the dog paddock. It is easy to assume that all dogs like to be stroked as we perceive it as a friendly gesture, but for dogs like Maia any physical contact from a stranger can be threatening and intrusive. Maia had become so used to being completely passive when humans did anything to her, she would lower her head, half close her eyes and completely shut down until the interaction was over. I was determined to ensure that I never saw her react in that way again. I had to work round Maia rather than expect her to fit in with me. Right from day one she would start to learn that she was safe and that she had control over what happened to her. Desperate as I was to stroke her, I knew that she wasn't ready for it. I would have to be patient and wait until she invited me to touch her. I was not going to rush the process. It could take days or weeks but the ball was firmly in Maia's court. In the meantime I still had my hairy hippo to stroke and he does give the most amazing hugs.

Another half hour passed and then I saw Maia briefly stick her head up from behind the arm of the sofa and quickly duck down again. OMG! Did that just really happen?! This was great. She was already learning about her new home from the safety of her den. I tried to ignore it but I got a strong sense that I was being watched! Maia was learning from and scrutinising my every move.

I felt by this time Maia must be starting to get hungry so I went to the fridge to get some chicken. As I walked past the edge of her den, without looking at Maia or saying anything to her, I dropped a few little pieces of chicken on the floor then continued on to the sofa and sat down. This enabled Maia to eat the chicken in her own time without any pressure from me. After a few seconds she reached out of her den, had a good sniff and then tentatively ate the chicken. This was great. When dogs are excessively stressed they refuse to eat as their body is preparing them to fight the perceived threat or to run away. This is called 'fight or flight response'. As the body prepares itself for action the gastrointestinal system slows down and inhibits appetite. As Maia took the chicken so readily, it seemed like she was beginning to be a little less defensive. It was also a great sign as it seemed that she was actually quite fond of food!

The next hour or so was spent with me sitting quietly on the sofa with Tam at my feet. Occasionally I would throw a little chicken onto the floor by Maia's den and each time she would reach out and gobble it up. I was still being careful not to look at her or talk to her so she realised that I was the provider of nice things without asking anything of her. Then the biggest shock of all ... About three hours after Tammy and Karen had left and to my absolute amazement, Maia slunk out of her den and climbed up on to the sofa with me! She immediately lay down curled up in a tight very tense ball at the far end and watched me with wide, mistrusting eyes. I could barely contain my delight and excitement but it was so important that I remained calm and completely ignored her. I hadn't expected Maia to venture out from her den at all that day and I didn't expect to be joined on the sofa for several days. Maia had certainly surprised me - the first of many.

I put her rapid ascent onto the sofa almost entirely down to healing. It is an incredibly powerful yet gentle tool that quickly instils trust and confidence in animals. The healing energy made it very clear to Maia what my intentions were. It helped me communicate to her that she was safe and loved, and that she had nothing to fear.

As the afternoon passed, I noticed Maia's eyes start to soften and the tension in her face ease. Tam kept walking over to her, sniffed her and then quietly walked away. Every time he did, I gave him loads of praise so he knew he was doing the right thing. Maia was a bit weird looking with her strange pointy nose, smelt funny and certainly didn't act like a normal dog. Tam wanted to learn all about her but he also instinctively knew that she needed time and space

The events of the day had clearly caught up with Maia and a short time after she joined me on the sofa she fell asleep. It was so lovely seeing her at peace. I watched her as she was sleeping. I started to familiarise myself with her pretty features, her body shape, her lumps and bumps and her scars. I watched her breathing pattern, inspected her patchy coat and her strange bony tail. I could even see her heartbeat just behind her left elbow. I felt so much love for this little hound and felt so protective towards her even though we barely knew each other. I knew at that moment that I had absolutely done the right thing in bringing her home.

EIGHT - Getting to know you

There was so much I had to learn about Maia. Her likes and dislikes, her wants and needs, and those triggers that tapped into the traumas of her past. Then there were aspects of her personality that would disclose *who* she really was. As Maia was so shut-down, it was difficult to determine any personality traits. Through the healing I felt that she was a really sweet soul, gentle, desperately trying to trust but there was something else. I felt that there was a cheeky side to this little hound, a sense of humour that was buried deep within. It was my mission to help Maia become who she was meant to be. I had a hunch that this shrinking violet had another side and I couldn't wait to unlock it.

By late afternoon I had yet another shock. As I was sitting on the sofa quietly watching the television, I felt a light poke on my leg. It was Maia! She had reached out her exceptionally long legs and poked me with one of her claws. I looked at her from the corner of my eye and saw her huge dark eyes looking up at me. This was Maia's invitation for me to touch her. I hadn't expected this moment to come for days, yet after just a few hours she had plucked up the courage to initiate contact. Fighting back the tears and trying to be 'professional', I gave Maia one light little stroke on her left shoulder with the back of my hand and then took my hand away. I touched her shoulder as most dogs can tolerate being touched in this area. It is not too sensitive and is far less intrusive than touching the sensitive head or face. I could see Maia's muscles were tense and she flinched when I touched her but she maintained her gaze. What was really wonderful was that she seemed to accept my touch which was incredibly humbling.

It was amazing feeling Maia's sleek silky coat for the first time. I had been waiting for this moment since the day I met her and I will never forget the sense of privilege I had. Then the ball was back in Maia's court. Would she ask me to stroke her again or had it been too much too soon? A few seconds later I received another poke on my leg. Again I reached across slowly and gave Maia one little stroke on her shoulder and then took my hand away. I wanted her to be the one in the driving seat. It was such an important lesson for her. Maia was realising that she had a voice - even though at this stage it was just a whisper - and I was ready to listen.

Before long I was stroking Maia's neck and shoulder. I was finding out which areas she liked to be touched and which areas she didn't. I was trying to gauge how firmly she liked to be stroked and scratched and in which direction. I quickly found a spot on her neck where she really enjoyed a good scratch. All the time I watched her reaction very closely. She made it clear from her posture and facial expression whether she liked what I was doing or not. If she liked it, her eyes started to close a little, she raised her nose slightly and she leant into my hand. If she didn't like it, she opened her eyes, fidgeted and looked away. I kept stopping at frequent intervals to make sure that Maia was in control of the interaction. Every time I stopped, she made it clear she wanted me to continue by giving me another poke. In no time at all Maia had trained me in the art of neck scratches. While I was gently stroking Maia with my right hand I was also giving Tam a rather more vigorous stroke - come shake - of his scruff with my left hand. They couldn't be more at odds in what they liked. It was a bit like rubbing your belly with one hand while tapping your head with the other! This was something I was going to have to work on!

Before Maia had completely filled up on chicken it was supper time. I made Tam's supper first with his special hypoallergenic food and then opened the brand new bag of food that I had ordered specially for Maia and sprinkled a few bits of chicken on top to whet her appetite. I had intended to feed them both in the kitchen but as Maia was starting to settle on the sofa I felt it would be best to feed her there just for today. I put Tam's food down first and he started to tuck in. I wanted to help him be secure in his new big brother role. He had been here longest so he should get his supper first. Then I put Maia's bowl next to her on the sofa and walked back into the kitchen so she could eat in peace.

As I watched Maia eat from a discrete distance I noticed that she picked all the pieces of chicken off the top before leaving the rest of her food. So much for feeding her something familiar! When Maia had made it clear she didn't want any more I quickly removed her bowl. Her food wasn't a hypoallergenic variety and would be like kryptonite to Tam. If he got hold of it, we would both pay for it in the night! Hopefully Maia would be a little more enthusiastic about eating her breakfast.

Maia had now been with me for about nine hours so I felt it was time to take a trip to the garden. She had spent a very long time in kennels and I had been told that there had been 'toileting issues' when she had previously been rehomed. I felt that it would be best to go back to basics and assume that Maia had never been taught to go out into the garden to toilet. There was just one tiny problem - Maia was terrified of my garden!

My garden was a decent size and had a good solid fence round it but it was a slightly odd 'dog-leg' shape. To get to the garden you had to walk down a short passageway, which then opened up and stretched down to the left. My garden was also surrounded on all sides by my neighbours' gardens and despite being screened, you can hear them talking in their gardens. This could be an issue.

In order not to damage our new-found but still very shaky new friendship, I felt it was important that Maia went out to the garden by choice and under her own steam rather than be forced out on the lead. First I thought I'd head out to the garden with Tam. He loved the garden and bounded outside with his usual enthusiasm and I hoped that would give Maia confidence to join us. Admittedly that was wishful thinking, it was never going to be that easy!

Luckily, despite having a belly full of supper Maia did have a little room left for a bit more chicken. I now know that however full she is, Maia will *always* have room for a bit more chicken! I returned to the cottage, encouraged Maia off the sofa in her own time and rewarded her with chicken for every tiny attempt she made to come with me. This was quite successful and very slowly we made our way through the kitchen, out the back door and along the passageway to the garden. As we reached the garden, Maia tentatively poked her nose around the corner to take a look.

Unfortunately, just as she did she heard my lovely neighbours talking quietly in their garden. With that, she spun round and bolted back into the cottage and hid in her den. Her reaction was a stark reminder of how fearful she was. I decided that she could probably hold her bladder for a few more hours so I would work on strengthening our relationship with neck scratches and strokes and try the garden again later. At this stage the priority was to build trust and positive experiences. It also bought me some more thinking time.

Tam had been so patient and restrained with Maia, that I felt he deserved some special 1-2-1 time with me where he could let off some steam. Tam is really gentle and sensitive but he is also a real BOY! He loves to play rough and tumble games where he throws himself all over the place with this big silly toothy grin on his face. One of his signature moves is to run at top speed down the garden, drop a shoulder and do a full body roll. It's scary to watch but Tam enjoys it and doesn't usually hurt himself so it seems a shame to stop him. We had a lovely game and once Tam had worn me out, we returned to the cottage.

Maia was still lying on the sofa watching the television so I thought it was a good time to make myself some dinner. While I was in the kitchen preparing my meal I also kept an eye on Maia. She didn't seem particularly worried about the sound of plates, saucers and cutlery rattling or cupboard doors opening and closing. She didn't even react when I boiled my extremely noisy kettle. It was all very encouraging. She was much more concerned about where I was than what I was doing.

Suddenly out of nowhere Maia leapt off the sofa and ran round the living room in a complete panic. Her tail was clamped down between her legs and she didn't know where to go. After a couple of laps she ran into her den and stood at the back looking very scared and trembling from head to toe. That was a pretty extreme reaction! What on earth could have triggered that response? I couldn't see anything obvious so my attention turned to the TV. Maia reacted during an advert where a man had been whistling. Could whistling be a trigger from her past or was it the tone of his voice? I was aware that Maia was very fearful of men but she hadn't reacted to men on the TV before this incident. Perhaps she had been frightened by a man who whistled or sounded like the man in the advert? The next time the advert played I would be watching her reaction very closely.

It was really hard for me to reassure Maia as we were still only just starting to get to know each other. I knew that if I approached her, far from reassuring her it could well make her even more scared. I felt so helpless. Then, without being asked, Tam walked over to Maia and just stood next to her. He didn't try and sniff her or get her to respond. He just offered her silent reassurance. It was amazing to watch. Scientists are forever arguing about animal sentience, about whether animals can experience emotions and whether they can sense emotions in others. Then here, right in front of me, Tam sensed that Maia was scared and needed reassurance and took matters into his own paws. Tam was already showing sensitivity towards Maia it was so much more than I could have hoped for. He was starting to get to know and understand who she was but doing so in a really gentle, kind, way. I felt so proud of him. After a couple of minutes Maia came out from her den and returned to her spot on the sofa. It had certainly been an interesting reaction.

After dinner I went back out to the garden for a game with Tam. All this tip-toeing around Maia was taking its toll and he needed to have some fun. We had a good game of rough and tumble where

Tam contorted himself into the most unnatural positions whilst I grabbed the scruff of his neck and gave it a good shake. It doesn't sound much like fun but to Tam it is the best game *ever*! After he had thrown himself around for a while he seemed much calmer. We sat on the grass surrounded by a selection of his favourite toys, which he always brings out with him and never takes back in. That was my job. Sometimes I question which one of us is the retriever.

We watched the sun setting behind the trees and enjoyed the peace until it started to get a bit too chilly. We went back inside to find Maia in exactly the same spot on the sofa. I think she had taken the opportunity to catch up on some sleep after what must have been an incredibly long and stressful day.

I felt it would be good if we all had an early night. Maia was settled on the sofa so I decided that it would be sensible for us to sleep downstairs just for this first night. She had spent the whole day on the sofa except for fleeing briefly to her den, so it was looking like she had chosen the sofa to be her safe place. Of course, you know what that meant - Maia and Tam would sleep on the sofa and I would be sleeping on the floor!

There was just one little issue. It was now 10pm and Maia hadn't had a wee since she arrived that morning. Her bladder must have been close to bursting. Somehow, I had to try and get her out into the garden. This could be quite a challenge!

By this time of night the garden was always really peaceful and quiet except for owls calling and the odd bark or should I say 'scream' of the muntjac deer. As soon I opened the back door Tam bounded outside. He always liked to check that everything was in order in the garden before he went to bed, patrolling round the perimeter and marking his territory. By stark contrast Maia didn't seem in any hurry to venture out again. I encouraged her off the sofa and through the kitchen, rewarding her with chicken. She was trying so hard. I can only imagine how challenging it must have been for her to trust me. Then just as Maia walked out through the back door Tam spotted something and started barking. The timing couldn't have been worse! In a flash Maia turned, bolted back into the cottage and jumped onto the sofa. My heart sank. I looked at Maia who was now tightly curled in a tense ball. After all the time I had spent encouraging her out into the garden it looked like we were back to square one. Thanks Tam.

It was so tempting to pick Maia up and carry her outside or to clip on her lead and make her go outside but I knew that would undo all the progress she had made. It would be easy to overpower her and force her to go out but that's not how I work. Maia was just starting to trust me. If I forced her outside I would betray her trust, just like all the other humans who hadn't listened to her fears. What was the worst that could happen if Maia didn't go out? She would toilet in the house. It wasn't ideal but I could clean it up. On balance it was definitely a better option than destroying the fragile trust that had been built. I decided to leave toilet training for another day and instead focussed on helping Maia feel safe.

I started to prepare for an uncomfortable night on the floor and brought my bedding downstairs. As soon as Maia saw me coming into the room with my arms full she leapt off the sofa and ran to her den with her tail between her legs. Seeing her reaction I put my bedding down at the far end of the room and gave her plenty of time to have a good look at it. She certainly seemed worried about me approaching with my arms full. Perhaps this was another trigger. Had someone thrown something at her or dropped something on her? After a few minutes she climbed back up onto the sofa. I would wait until she had settled again before making up my makeshift 'bed' on the floor. Maia watched me very closely but held firm on her position on the sofa.

After a quick tidy round I got myself ready for bed. I gave Tam his goodnight treat and offered Maia another little piece of chicken which she took readily. Finally I made up my 'bed' and settled down for the night.

Maia fell asleep almost immediately on the comfy sofa and Tam settled on the floor right next to her. He was definitely going to look after Maia on her first night in her new home. I looked up at Maia and she looked so peaceful. I felt all the inevitable sacrifices and challenges that lay ahead were worth it. Never again would this little hound spend another night in a kennel. Maia was home. Forever.

As I lay in 'bed' I recalled all the day's events. There were two important lessons I had learned about Maia that day. First, she loved her food and second, she really appreciated home comforts. These insights could prove very handy over the coming days and weeks.

NINE ~ A new dawn, a new day, a new life

It was a long and sleepless night. Not for Maia, she slept like a log and didn't move at all! My mind however was whirring - all night. At about 5.30am she started to stir and after a few minutes she got off the sofa and had a good stretch. It was getting light, the birds were singing - and Maia must have been absolutely bursting! It was time to seize the moment and try and encourage her outside again.

I wasn't sure how she would respond to me. I was expecting to have to go back to the beginning and reacquaint myself to her but to my amazement I was able to pick up from where we had left off. What a brave girl. Armed with a fistful of chicken I started to encourage Maia towards the back door. She was very tense and cautious as she made her way through the kitchen. Just as she got outside to the passage-way she could hold on no more and the floodgates opened. Maia had managed to hold on for about 17 hours, which was really impressive but she couldn't hold on forever!

The key to Maia's toilet training was to make it very clear what I wanted and to praise and reward her for doing the right thing. The moment she wee'd I gave her loads of praise so she had no doubt that what she was doing was right. The moment she had finished she turned and rushed back into the cottage and onto the sofa. I gave her loads of chicken to reward her for toileting outside. It was definitely a positive and rewarding experience for Maia and hopefully one that she would remember.

The morning after Maia's arrival was beautifully bright and sunny. The birds were singing and it was the perfect start to the day. To top it all, I had the luxury of a completely empty diary so the focus of the day would be to hang out with Maia and Tam and give us all time to learn more about each other. Tam took it upon himself to make the first move and wish Maia a good morning. He went straight up to her and thrust his big fat golden retriever muzzle in her face. Whilst it was a friendly gesture, Maia was clearly intimidated by his approach. She raised her head, leant back into the sofa and tried to get away from him. Oh dear, that wasn't the response Tam had expected. He seemed quite put out that his house guest didn't want to talk to him so he walked away towards his bed. Seeing Tam's reaction I quickly called him over to me to give him some reassurance. It's still early days fella. Just give her a bit more time.

It was with a little trepidation that I sat down on the sofa next to Maia that morning. I had no idea how she would react to me, so I made no attempt to talk to her, touch her or even look at her. It must have been very strange and disorientating for her waking up in a home instead of her kennel. I always imagine how hard it must be for any animal in a new home. It must be unimaginably scary for them not knowing what was going to happen to them in the next minute, the next hour, the next day or who they were going to meet. For a fearful dog like Maia it must be absolutely terrifying.

As I quietly took my place on the sofa, I avoided making direct eye contact with Maia but watched her reaction closely out of the corner of my eye. I was looking for any tiny movement or signal that would let me gauge how she was coping. I could feel her gaze was also fixed on me. It was definitely a case of you, watching me, watching you. She was certainly extremely tense and her posture quite defensive, but she held her spot on the sofa and didn't try to jump off or bolt to her den. That was definitely a great sign. Maia's desire for comfort outweighed her fear of me.

Tam was more of a concern. He quietly took up position on his bed over the other side of the room, lay with his muzzle resting on his front paws and looked up at us through the tops of his eyes. He looked so lost and sad. This was such a huge change for him. In the mornings Tam usually had my undivided attention. We would have a bit of a game and he would sit by my feet and have a stroke. Now he felt left out and confused. He was already making sacrifices for Maia yet far from being best friends, she had made it pretty clear that she didn't want anything to do with him. This could be tricky.

In those quiet moments in the early hours when I was planning for Maia's arrival, I had hoped they would hit it off from the moment she arrived. Sadly it wasn't going to be that easy. Their relationship was going to take work. Little did I realise just how much work.

I didn't want Tam to build up any resentment towards Maia at this stage and it broke my heart to see him so sad. I had to jump in and do something. I called him over to me and we had a good cuddle which was lovely but true to form it quickly deteriorated to a rough-and-tumble game. After a good battle Tam seemed much happier and more relaxed.

Maia had watched our game without getting overly worried by it despite me waving my arms around, playing rough with Tam. Up to that point I had tried to keep my movements quite small and slow so as not to startle her, but by observing from a safe distance she had coped really well. Tam's reaction would hopefully show her that humans can make strange noises and sudden movements without it being a threat to her. Maia was at the beginning of a very steep learning curve.

I felt the dogs needed a positive distraction so I decided to give them some breakfast. I had planned to feed both Tam and Maia in the kitchen but my kitchen is quite small and Maia was still very uneasy about it. To help her feel safe when she was eating I decided to feed her in the living room where she found it familiar. It is advisable to feed sighthounds and large breed dogs from raised food bowls as they can be prone to a serious condition called 'bloat' if they eat from a bowl on the floor. In preparation I had a box ready as a bowl stand for Maia. Unfortunately, when I put it on the floor Maia wouldn't go near it - not even for food. I had to improvise so I grabbed a selection of Tam's toys, stacked them up like a Jenga tower and balanced Maia's food bowl on the top. Rather cautiously, Maia approached her bowl and started to pick at her food. It did the job but I would definitely have to find a more permanent solution.

It was slightly disappointing to see that Maia wasn't tucking into her breakfast. I wasn't sure if she was just wary of her surroundings or if there was something else going on. Perhaps she still had a full belly after eating all that chicken the previous day, or perhaps she was unsure about eating from the rather unconventional soft toy tower. I decided to monitor her appetite over the next few days to see if it picked up once she'd had more time to settle in.

When Maia finished eating she returned to the safety of the sofa. I removed her bowl then joined her on the sofa where she was quick to nudge me for a scratch. Following her excellent tutoring the night before, I knew exactly where she wanted me to stroke her. I took the 'less is more' approach and started with a short, light stroke on her neck with the back of my hand. Once again she jumped when she felt my touch but she seemed happy for me to continue. It was so important at this stage to make sure that my behaviour was totally predictable for Maia. Whenever I went to stroke her, I always followed the same pattern so she was always ready for the next stage. This was essential to help her build her confidence and trust in me. Tam had decided to take up position on the floor by the sofa beneath where Maia was lying. I wasn't quite sure if he lay there to be close to her or if he did it to keep an eye on her. Either way there was certainly no way that Maia would be able to do *anything* without Tam knowing about it!

After spending some time with Maia it was 'Tam time' - time when I would give Tam my complete undivided attention. He loved the garden so after collecting several of his toys in his mouth, Tam led the way outside. It was really lovely spending time with him. I felt so protective towards him. He was here first and had such a special place in my heart, it was crucial that he grew to love his new house mate. We had a good game then we sat quietly on the grass half way down the garden where I sent Tam some healing. It was such a special time. I felt that he was confused and needed comfort and reassurance. He really didn't understand how to interact with Maia. He had been doing everything right during his polite interactions yet she had snubbed him at every attempt. It reminded me just how important it was to monitor Tam closely. On the outside he seemed fine, his normal goofy thuggish self, but on the inside he was definitely struggling.

As the weather was so lovely, it felt like the perfect opportunity to spend the day sitting outside. Tam and I could relax and enjoy some quality time together and Maia would have plenty of time to venture into the garden on her own terms. I was usually so busy with work, it was a real luxury to be able to just sit in the sunshine with Tam and enjoy spending some quiet time together.

I kept popping in to check on Maia at regular intervals. Each time she was just as I had left her, lying on the sofa listening to Classic FM. It was quite a change from her kennel life just 24 hours earlier. I knew she couldn't hurt herself on anything, so I left her alone. That way she could have a good look round from the safety of the sofa without having to worry about what Tam or I were doing. I knew that if I gave Maia enough time and space, she would eventually be confident enough to venture off the sofa and investigate her new home. It had to be her choice.

By late morning, it seemed that curiosity finally got the better of her. As Tam and I were sitting on the grass and relaxing, something compelled me to look up and I was treated to a fabulous sight. Maia's little face was peering round the corner by the passageway, watching us. This was a monumental development as it was the first time that Maia had been brave enough to come out of her own accord. She was so scared of the garden it must have taken a lot of courage for her to venture out. I could see the strain and tension in her face from the far end of the garden. Every muscle in her body was tight and she was on high alert, poised to bolt at any moment. She didn't stay out for long. After the briefest of glances, her new-found confidence deserted her and she turned and quickly ran back into the cottage. It might only have been a brief glimpse outside but it was a huge milestone. I stayed out in the garden with Tam. Maia would come out again when she was ready.

I would find out how difficult it had been for Maia to dare herself to go outside based on the length of time it took before she tried again. If her confidence hadn't been too badly dented, it wouldn't be long before she re-appeared. If she had frightened herself the first time it might be some time before she plucked up enough courage to try again. Thankfully I only had to wait for a few minutes before her face appeared. As before, she only stayed for a couple of seconds before rushing back inside but this was hugely encouraging.

To help boost Maia's confidence I always made sure that she had a clear escape route back to her place of safety. Knowing that she could return to the cottage at any time would encourage her to be a bit braver and go out and explore. The only way I could ensure this was to leave the back door wide open during the day until Maia felt safe and confident in the garden. This was likely to take weeks. I just had to accept that I would be living with a refreshing draught blowing through the cottage for a while and to dress accordingly. Oh well, it could have been worse. It could have been February!

Throughout the rest of the morning, Maia paid frequent visits to the garden, staying out a few seconds longer each time before bolting back inside. As her confidence grew she gradually started to make her way a little further down the garden and started to sniff the air and take in her surroundings before losing her nerve and rushing back inside again. It was lovely watching her dare herself to stay out for just a little bit longer. She was such a brave little hound.

Tam was very keen to show Maia around. He quietly walked with her as she started to familiarise herself with the garden, giving her the confidence to explore. I could see that he really wanted to play with her but he contained his excitement and was careful not to crowd her. It was so lovely to watch them together. Tam was trying so hard. Something that immediately struck me was that Maia's posture had already started to change. Up until this point I had only ever seen really apologetic, fearful posture from Maia with her back tense and her tail clamped down between her legs and yet now there was already a noticeable change. Maia was starting to carry her tail out behind her. She looked a little less anxious and less tense. As she started to investigate the garden Maia pricked up her fabulous houndy radar ears and listened to the new sounds that surrounded her. It is amazing how different she looked with her ears almost standing up on end. Sighthounds have such a vast range of ear positions and facial expressions, it was a joy to see a little glimpse of her character start to show through all the tension. As she walked round the garden, she frequently stopped to sniff the air. She pointed her long pointy nose skyward and squinted her eyes in the glare of the sun. She looked a picture.

I couldn't have been more delighted with her progress. She would rush inside at the slightest noise but she was getting better and better as the day went on. If something spooked her, she quickly regained her confidence and tentatively ventured back out again. We had a *looong* way to go but the early signs were encouraging.

After a really positive afternoon it was supper time. I hoped that Maia had built up a good appetite after spending so much time exploring the garden. As before, I gave Tam his supper first and then built the Jenga tower of toys. I put Maia's food on the top and she started to tuck in. Great! It must just have been first night nerves that stopped her from eating her kibble the night before. I tried to play it cool and avoided watching her too closely as she ate but the anticipation was killing me. My relief was short-lived. As soon as Maia had picked out all the chicken and nice wet meaty bits, she left all the kibble in her bowl again and returned to the sofa. Not so great. I gave her a bit more of the wet dog food and she immediately gobbled it down. Despite Maia making it pretty clear to me which food she preferred, I decided to persevere with her kibble for a couple of days and then review. You can't knock my optimism!

After they had finished supper I took Tam back out into the garden for some quality 1-2-1 time. After a good game we made our way back into the kitchen. As I looked across into the living room I just caught sight of a soft toy flying through the air. Now I didn't see her do it but there could only have been one explanation. By the time we had walked through the kitchen, Maia was back up on the sofa lying in her usual position as if nothing had happened. This little hound definitely had a playful side and I couldn't wait to see more of it.

I didn't have to wait long. About an hour later I went back out with Tam. We were sitting at the top of the garden having a nice game with Kermit, one of Tam's favourite soft toys, then like a torpedo Maia flew out of the passageway, grabbed Kermit from right under our noses and ran back indoors with it. It all happened so fast I don't think Tam or I really knew what was happening. After months with just a little teddy to play with, Maia was taking full advantage of this soft toy bonanza. This timid fearful hound had some front. Perhaps I should re-name her 'Fagin'.

 As our first full day together drew to a close, I opened the back door so the dogs could go out in the garden and empty. After a little hesitation, Maia went out and joined Tam. By now it was quite dark outside yet that really didn't seem to faze Maia at all. I guess she had got used to the dark when living in kennels. She spent a couple of minutes pottering around the garden and then she toileted before rushing back inside to the safety of the sofa. I gave her loads of praise and a tasty reward to show her that she had done the right thing.

As Maia seemed quite settled, I felt that she was ready to spend the night upstairs. This was particularly good news, not just in terms of Maia's progress - I was really looking forward to sleeping in my own bed again. I decided to allow access to upstairs about an hour before bed time to give Maia enough time to find the confidence to go upstairs and have a bit of a look round before settling down. If Tam and I went upstairs, Maia could follow in her own time. If she preferred to stay downstairs, she was welcome to do so. Her choice.

I switched off the lights and turned to go up the stairs but I was beaten to it by Tam with Maia in hot pursuit. Far from being too scared to go upstairs, she had no intention of being left behind. By the time I made it up the stairs, Maia had already curled up right in the middle of my bed! As she looked so comfortable, my first thought was to allow her to sleep there. My previous lurcher used to sleep on my bed without any problems after all. Then I looked across at Tam. I'll never forget the look on his face. He looked absolutely devastated. I had never allowed him on my bed as he was way too big, hairy and smelly. It had never been an issue as he was quite happy sleeping in his own bed at the foot of mine, but I could tell by the look on his face that I could never allow Maia to stay on my bed. It just wouldn't be fair. There was just one little problem. Maia had found her perfect spot to sleep and she wasn't going to give it up lightly.

I tried coaxing Maia off the bed. No chance. She just curled up into a tighter ball. I sat on the bed next to her and hoped she would get the hint. Nope. There was only one thing I knew that Maia valued perhaps even more than her chosen spot on my bed. I went downstairs to the fridge, grabbed some chicken and went back upstairs. As soon as Maia smelt the chicken she knew I meant business. She climbed off my bed and stepped into her own very comfortable bed, turned a couple of circles before slumping down in quite dramatic fashion. I felt like reminding Maia where she had been sleeping just 48 hours earlier as it certainly wasn't as comfortable as her new bed. While it might not have been her first choice, it was still a significant upgrade! I gave her the chicken and looked across to Tam. He looked much happier and settled down to sleep.

Despite being her second choice, Maia's bed clearly met with her approval as when I woke the next morning, she was in exactly the same position she had adopted the night before. She hadn't moved an inch. Result.

Day 1 ~ Finding her feet

Day 2 ~ very unsure of the garden but ...

... taking a lead from Tam

TEN - Day 3

A couple of days had passed and I was starting to learn a bit about *who* Maia was. I learnt that she was a reasonably early riser. Her internal alarm clock went off at 7.10am. As soon as she woke she had a stretch and then thrust her front legs onto my bed so that she towered over me, then poked my face repeatedly with her nose until I got up. It was a pretty full-on wakeup call. It was a bit like someone shouting 'WAKE UP' in my ear through a loud hailer but I didn't mind a bit. It was amazing that Maia was confident enough to interact with me in that way after less than 48 hours together. It was wonderful to see her so excited and animated. She definitely woke ready to seize the day.

In order to keep everything predictable for Maia, I kept to the same routine. First thing was to go out in the garden and wait for her to have a wee. And wait ... and wait ... this could take time. I knew that she was capable of holding her bladder for and eye-watering 17 hours but I was happy to give her all the time she needed. I really wanted to set her up for success right from the beginning. It was important that I stayed outside with Maia as I needed to be sure that she had actually emptied and it also meant that I could praise and reward her the moment she toileted outside.

What was really interesting to me was that in the early days, Maia didn't seem to have any concept of rewards or how to get them. I know that she received plenty of praise in the past from kennel staff and Forever Hounds Trust volunteers but she was too shut down to enjoy it. She had to learn what praise meant and understand that she could *earn* rewards. As a positive reinforcement trainer, this was really strange to me. Most dogs catch on quickly that if they do the desired behaviour, they get a reward. Maia wasn't most dogs!

I was extremely careful to keep my behaviour consistent and pre-dictable. I kept my voice calm and quiet and avoided making sudden movements. As she became more confident I would be able to shake things up a bit. I was also very careful where I positioned myself in relation to where she was. Maia was really wary when I was moving around the cottage so I always gave her as much room as possible so she never felt trapped. I also ensured that she always had clear access to an escape route. Maia was already starting to grow in confidence but I was aware that she was on a bit of a knife edge. She was tentatively building her confidence but it was still very fragile. Any error of judgement on my part could set her back.

Maia's automatic reaction was always to back away from anything she was unsure of. If Tam or I approached her she would immediately back away, but she would never turn her back on us. She always needed to be able to see what we were doing. If we needed to get past her, she would back away until we passed and then happily follow close behind - sometimes even stepping on my heels - but if I turned towards her she would back away again. I really wanted Maia to learn that she didn't have to fear us and that she could stand her ground.

To teach Maia that approaching me was a good thing, I immediately called her to me whenever I saw her back away. I stood slightly side on to her and avoided direct eye contact to make myself as non-threatening as possible, and when she approached me I gave her loads of praise and a food reward. I was confident that in time she would relax around me but that was some way off yet.

Maia's fear response was so automatic that she didn't have time to think and rationalise. It was just a case of 'if in doubt... RUN!' It was quicker, easier and safer for her to go straight into survival mode and flee rather than waste valuable seconds thinking about it. I wanted to help her remain calm and start thinking about how she interacted with me - and eventually to other people. Although she might never completely forget the fear, I could certainly teach her new ways to respond when she was unsure, and give her positive experiences to overshadow her previous unhappy memories.

I was definitely starting to see glimpses of Maia's personality and she was not without her idiosyncrasies. If she spotted a fly or a spider on the wall, she was completely transfixed. She would stare at it for hours if I didn't remove it. Now I didn't mind sending the flies on their way but the spiders were a different matter! One afternoon Maia spotted a spider walking across the living room wall. This wasn't just any spider, oh no, this was a massive house spider that was the size or a tarantula and Maia couldn't take her eyes off it. Now that I'd spotted it neither could I! I couldn't sit and watch it with the same unwavering intrigue as Maia. I grabbed a plastic measuring jug and a piece of card, took a deep breath, then bravely removed the spider and relocated it to the garden. Maia's trance-like state abated but I knew she was already looking for the next spider to fixate on.

Flies often met with a slightly more messy fate. If one landed within Maia's reach she would watch it for a while before attempting to catch it. Unfortunately for the fly, she was very clumsy about it.

While her tenacity was to be commended, she did have a pretty high failure rate. If she managed to catch one she would take it in her mouth then spit it out, take it in her mouth and spit it out again. In the end we would be left with a soggy and slightly maimed fly crawling around on the carpet and it would be up to me to put it out of its misery.

Maia also had an obsession with feathers. If she found a feather in the garden she was absolutely delighted with it. She would toss it in the air and pounce on it and then carry it around with her as if it was the best thing in the world. I can only imagine her obsession with flies and spiders resulted from spending so long in kennels with little stimulation. Feathers that blew into her run must have held a similar attraction, something new that broke the monotony of kennel life. I felt that Maia's fly, spider and feather obsession would gradually decline as she found other more appropriate ways to amuse herself such as playing with toys or, fingers crossed, Tam.

As I was starting to get to know Maia I was also starting to let my guard down when I was around her - big mistake! It was lunchtime so I made myself a cheese sandwich. Tam had never really been very interested in food, which is unusual for a golden retriever. They are often quite obsessed with food and have a reputation for being great hoovers. Tam was different. I knew that if I left any food around - even on the floor in front of him - he would never dream of taking it. The problem was it wasn't just me and Tam anymore.

Maia was curled up in her usual spot as I brought my sandwich in. I realised that I had left my drink in the kitchen, so I placed my lunch on the arm of the sofa and went back into the kitchen to get it. The distance from sofa to kitchen is about four metres. After retrieving my drink and returning to the living room, I arrived in time to see Maia wrapping her long skinny jaws around my sandwich! I must only have been out the room for three seconds! I said her name, which was enough to interrupt the theft and Maia reluctantly spat it out. I quietly said 'a-aa' to her to let her know that I didn't really want her to repeat that behaviour and she returned to her seat. I was careful during the correction to keep my voice really soft and calm to make sure I didn't frighten her but I did want to let her know that I would prefer it if she didn't steal my food. No harm done and a lesson learnt - for both of us.

I really should have known better, it was a rookie mistake. A little part of me was also quite chuffed that Maia was confident enough to carry out such a behaviour right under my nose. The audacity of it! As for the sandwich - those with a weak disposition please jump to next paragraph - I have to admit that I took it back to the kitchen, cut it in half, threw away the half with the teeth marks in it and ate the rest. Well, it seemed a shame to waste it. I can't say I enjoyed it very much though. Note to self - never leave food unattended around Maia. It will dramatically reduce its 'best before' date!

After lunch I went out into the garden with Tam, sat on the grass and waited for Maia to come out and join us. As before, she kept to a similar pattern of behaviour. Venture out into the garden, have a look around, get spooked and then run back inside. Repeat! When she was outside there was definitely a change in her burgeoning relationship with Tam. They were starting to be more confident around each other and interacted more. If one found a blade of grass of particular interest, the other would come over and take a closer look. Tam was familiar with every blade of grass in the garden so it seemed that he was going along with Maia to help develop a social and emotional connection with her.

It had been another really beautiful afternoon and the dogs had made great progress. After several hours hanging out, we returned inside. Maia immediately went to the sofa, but this time instead of lying in the far corner, she lay right in the middle taking up all three seats so there was no room for Tam or me to join her. Sighthound breeds are all legs, capable of curling up into a tiny ball and thus take up very little sofa space. Clearly Maia wasn't going to be one of those. Time to get a bigger sofa!

The time spent in the garden had clearly helped Tam and Maia to bond. Once back inside, Tam kept going up to her on the sofa to check she was ok and she responded by poking her long pointy nose right in his face. She certainly didn't have much respect for personal space and repeatedly poked his face quite sharply with her nose. Her movements were very fast compared to Tam's and he wasn't at all sure what to make of it. He didn't seem to understand that it was a friendly gesture, so he backed away and went to lay down, much to Maia's dismay. After a while Tam got up, strode over to Maia and did a lovely big play bow and gave a 'woof' inviting her to play. It was such a lovely gesture, almost like marching over to her and holding out his hand for a friendly and welcoming yet slightly over-enthusiastic hand shake, but unfortunately it didn't lead to the outcome he expected. Maia immediately took fright, leapt off the sofa and ran to her den. Poor Tam, he looked so confused and quietly made his way back to his bed.

It became apparent that there were significant communication issues between these two. They were both making lovely advances to each other and they had both performed some really friendly gestures but they were being completely misinterpreted. They are such different breeds and communicate in such different ways. It was as if they were speaking different languages. To top it all, I was stuck in the middle with my working knowledge of both, but neither my native tongue.

Each breed has traits and behaviours that we associate with that particular breed. The differences between golden retrievers and lurchers are quite significant. It was clear that Tam had to quickly learn 'lurcher' and Maia needed a crash course in 'golden retriever'. This wasn't going to be easy. I suddenly found myself in the role of 'canine translator'. How could I break the stalemate where Tam was defensive towards Maia and Maia was fearful of Tam?

It would be difficult to teach Maia to curb her nose-in-the-face behaviour as it is quite a normal behaviour for sighthounds to greet each other that way. I also had to be careful not to do anything that would make her hesitate before approaching Tam. I wanted to encourage friendly interactions between them. I decided to work on Tam. I had to teach him that being poked in the face by Maia was actually positive! If I could increase his tolerance perhaps he wouldn't be so defensive when Maia approached him. This was a big ask. I don't think I'd like it if someone came up to me and poked me in the face, with their nose or any other part of their anatomy.

Whenever Maia poked her pointy nose in Tam's face, I gave him loads of praise and reassurance. Instead of being worried by it, I hoped he would start to understand that it was intended as a friendly gesture. I was reasonably optimistic that in time I could change how Tam felt about these interactions. That Maia was just trying to make friends. This might be a long process!

Despite the obvious language barrier, there were some positive signs between the two dogs. Their walks round the garden were lovely to watch as Tam was giving Maia so much confidence. They also started to try and play in the living room. It was tentative and really awkward but at least they were trying. I threw a vetbed on the floor to mark out a comfortable play area. Tam was first to go over and lay down on it and after a little time Maia climbed off the sofa and lay on the vetbed next to him. Then they both got a bit stuck. It was like a young couple on their first date with neither knowing how to make the next move. Maia was the first to break the stalemate. She stretched out her legs and rested her muzzle on her front paws. This gesture took her a little closer to Tam. Tam mirrored her behaviour and did the same. After about 10 minutes, Maia made the next move and cautiously rolled onto her side which again took her slightly closer to Tam. He looked a bit uncomfortable but held his position. He had never had another dog try to snuggle up to him and get into his personal space before and he wasn't sure what to make of it. I tried to reassure him but shortly after, he got up and moved away from Maia. It was such a shame as it all seemed to be going so well.

I was quite surprised by Tam's reaction as he is such an affectionate dog with humans but cuddling up to another dog was new for him. After a short time Maia climbed back onto the sofa. My heart wept for them as they were both trying so hard but not really getting anywhere. Oh well, it was very early days and there would be many more opportunities.

Unfortunately, as with the greetings, their different play styles caused some issues. Tam likes to play rough. He likes to throw himself around and roll on the floor and with all that golden retriever padding, he never feels a thing. Maia on the other hand had a much more reserved play style and a much higher sense of self-preservation. She is built for speed and reclining on a sofa. She is not built for rough and tumble. Somehow, they were going to have to work out some mutual ground and develop a game that could be enjoyed equally by both. This was definitely easier said than done and judging from their early attempts, I really wasn't sure how they would ever be able to manage it.

ELEVEN - Day 4

Maia had been doing really well, way better than I could ever have hoped, but there was a problem looming. By this time Tam had been without a walk for three days. Cabin fever had set in and he was starting to climb the walls. Tam is a very good natured, laid back soul but if he doesn't get enough exercise his mood can quickly change and he becomes quite boisterous - and noisy. Tam has quite a loud, butch bark and when he barked, it frightened Maia. She was a bit intimidated by Tam anyway. Watching him barking, spinning and then flinging himself on the floor was doing nothing for her nerves - or mine! I had to get him out for a run. My problem was that whilst Maia was settling in really well in the cottage, she was still very jumpy in the garden. She certainly wasn't ready to venture beyond the garden fence and explore the big wide world. To further complicate matters, she couldn't be left home alone either. When I agreed to take her on I was advised that she needed the company of another dog in order to feel safe. It was definitely a dilemma. I was going to have to ask someone to come round and babysit for me. There was just one tiny problem. Maia was terrified of strangers!

In an ideal world I would have waited for a few more days before inviting someone round but I knew that Tam wouldn't be able to contain himself for much longer. My only option was to arrange for someone to pop round and help me teach Maia about visitors. She was very fearful of all strangers but was generally worse with men. I needed someone sensitive, quiet and gentle who wouldn't be offended by following all the instructions I would be offering. There was only one person it could be - my lovely neighbour Barb. She is a fellow healer, a lovely kind lady with beautiful energy. A quick phone call later, and the time was set. Barb would pop round later that afternoon.

I had to make sure that this visit was as easy as possible for Maia. She had her favourite spot on the sofa so it was important to leave that seat free for her should she feel confident enough to use it. I was also mindful not to leave anything blocking access to her den so she could bolt there at any time if she needed to. It would also be best if Barb didn't bring a coat or any bags with her as these were just something else for Maia to get frightened about. The plan was there wasn't really a plan! Barb would pop round for a short visit, quietly take a seat on the sofa and ignore Maia. We would see how Maia reacted and take things from there.

So, the time arrived. Before Barb had even had a chance to knock, Tam saw her through the window and started barking to alert me. As soon as all the commotion started, Maia leapt off the sofa and ran to her den. I'm not sure if it was Barb's arrival or Tam's barking that caused the reaction - probably a combination of the two - but Maia behaved absolutely as expected.

Tam frantically ran round the room collecting as many soft toys in his mouth as possible. Golden retrievers are gun dogs so they are predisposed to want to hold something in their mouths. Tam's personal best was seven large soft toys which was a sight to behold. Today was going to be an average day with just a modest three.

Since Tam was a puppy I had always taught him to sit when he went up to people. It meant that he has never jumped up at anyone. However, it also meant that when anyone tried to come into the cottage they had to get past him first. When sitting in position in full welcoming committee mode, Tam closely resembles an immovable roadblock that all visitors have a job to negotiate. Whilst not ideal for all visitors, Tam was the perfect distraction to divert attention away from Maia.

After a short time Barb managed to wrestle her way past him and took her seat on the sofa. Tam sat by her feet and I sat on the floor opposite the sofa so that Maia could keep an eye on me while I had a chat with Barb.

It didn't take long before curiosity started to get the better of Maia. She poked her head up from behind the arm of the sofa, took a look at Barb and then ducked back down again. I gave Maia reassurance and Barb ignored her brilliantly. After a while, Maia plucked up courage and came out of her den. She walked up to the sofa, took a look at Barb, then turned and returned to her den. I could see Maia was struggling with a predicament. She really wanted to come out and return to her nice safe, comfortable spot the sofa but that meant sharing it with Barb and she wasn't quite brave enough to risk it. Several times she walked to the sofa to assess the situation, took a good look then returned to her den. I could see she was getting frustrated. How dare Barb sit on her sofa!

After about half an hour, Maia came out of her den and took a good hard look. She walked to the sofa and went to lift a paw up as if to climb on but at the last moment nerves got the better of her. She had been so close, and given the extent of her anxiety, even contemplating joining a stranger on the sofa was an incredible effort.

After a short time Barb left. I had barely closed the door behind her when I heard Maia jumping back up onto the sofa. There certainly didn't seem to be any ill effects from Barb's visit. I didn't feel it would be long before Maia was bold enough to join visitors on the sofa. Like everything with Maia, it was just a matter of time.

We spent the rest of the afternoon in the garden. Maia was now staying out for several minutes at a time before something would frighten her and cause her to flee inside. For a short time she actually seemed like she was *enjoying* mooching around the garden with Tam. It was like her natural interest made her forget her fear until a noise or some movement from a neighbour's garden would trigger the sprint inside. She was still very tense but there were definitely subtle changes in her demeanour. She was starting to be a little more deliberate in her movement, walking with purpose if she caught a sniff in the air or saw something worth investigating. She was also holding her tail much higher and it was curled upwards like a proper lurcher. It almost looked like a big smile.

Then I saw it … Maia's tail wagged for the first time. It was just a glimpse that lasted barely two seconds but there was no mistaking it. It was definitely a wag! How fantastic! It was really emotional seeing that this sad little hound was starting to enjoy her new life.

Then out of the blue, Maia took off at top speed around the garden. It was like someone had suddenly hit her 'turbo boost' button. There were legs everywhere and Maia's skinny tail was flailing, acting like a rudder to try and keep her on her feet. It was hilarious! These frenetic outbursts of energy are known as 'zoomies' and it was wonderful to see Maia really enjoying herself and having such a great time. After two laps of the garden, she shot down the passage-way and disappeared back into the cottage.

I went inside to check on Maia and found her back on the sofa puffing like a steam train, trying to catch her breath. She was terribly unfit after spending such a long time in kennels with restricted exercise. It must have felt so amazing for her to be able to really run for the first time in many months but I had to be careful that she didn't overdo it. I was concerned that she could pull a muscle or strain a tendon. Then there was her heart which I could see pounding away to try and pump enough oxygen round her body. But she looked so happy. Her eyes were laughing and her tongue lolling as she tried to catch her breath. She was one happy little hound.

Despite my concerns it had been amazing to see her run like that. Her speed was incredible - much faster than Tam - even despite her frantic braking at each end of my garden necessary to make it round the corners. I could only imagine how wonderful it would be to see Maia run free in a big field when she got her fitness levels up. I couldn't wait for that day.

Tam was rather bemused by it all. As Maia was flying round the garden like a lunatic, he stood in the middle of the lawn as she shot past him, head up, tail up, not really knowing what to do. It was very exciting but she was just so fast! There was definitely more to this little hound. Far from being a scared, timid, attention grabber, perhaps she could be quite good fun after all.

We spent the rest of the afternoon in the garden with Maia gaining confidence by the minute. By the end of the afternoon she was staying out for greater lengths of time. Her tail was held up high and she was starting to really enjoy herself. I thought it was time to test her recall so I waited for her to go down to the bottom of the garden

Zoomies!

and then I called her name. She immediately bounded over to me and skidded to a halt just behind me. She looked so pleased with herself and kept poking me excitedly. I have to admit she put Tam's recall to shame. When I call Tam he always starts off with the best intention and gallops straight towards me but as he gets closer - perhaps only a few metres away - something always catches his eye which distracts him and then he then goes off on a tangent to see what it was. It is soooo frustrating! Maia seemed to have an excellent recall which would definitely come in very handy later on when we explored the big wide world.

Later that evening we were all relaxing in the cottage. Maia was still getting the hang of the sofa. She sometimes lay in gravity-defying positions with her legs and bottom hanging over the edge which always looked so precarious. Finally this evening gravity won. Maia was fast asleep, shifted a bit and fell off. Unfortunately, Tam was lying on the floor right next to the sofa and broke Maia's fall! They both had a very rude awakening and quite a fright but despite this Tam went straight over to Maia to check she was OK and reassure her. I couldn't believe how amazingly understanding Tam was. It was more than I ever could have wished for.

Part of my regular bedtime routine with Tam was that I would put a little bit of wet dog food in a plastic tray and give it to him when we went upstairs as a little bedtime treat. It didn't take Maia long to catch on. It was only a very small amount of meat but it made bedtimes *really* exciting.

As the evening of day four drew to a close I did all my usual late night checks. Doors locked, all appliances switched off, night light by the stairs switched on. I collected my phone and Tam's favourite teddy ready to take them upstairs. Before I had a chance to pick up the trays of meat and switch off the lights, Maia had already bolted up the stairs, scrambling to keep her footing in her rush to get there first. As I switched off the downstairs lights I could hear the thumping of lurcher feet on the floor above my head. What on earth was she doing up there?! Tam steadily made his way upstairs and as I rounded the corner at the bottom of the stairs, I saw a really wired wide-eyed pointy nosed little face peering round the bannister looking down at me. As I climbed the stairs, Maia was spinning in tight little circles in the middle of the floor before running back to the bannister again. Then she did a funny little shimmy, a lovely play bow, followed by another spin. Such excitement! It was absolutely wonderful to see her so animated. Her eyes were alive

69

with a really endearing little twinkle. I gave Tam his tray and as I walked across the room to Maia's late night snack spot she was bouncing up and down in anticipation. After months of kibble she certainly seemed to appreciate the finer things in life.

It didn't take Maia long to demolish her food then she ran over to where Tam had his tray. Tam was still eating so I quickly pointed out to Maia that I didn't think that it was such a good idea to poke her nose in his face at that particular moment. Tam is not possessive over food but he deserved to be able to eat his food in peace. Moments later Tam had finished his snack and went to Maia's tray to see if she had left anything. Maia seized the opportunity to check Tam's tray. Their optimism had to be admired as there was no way either of them would ever have left even the tiniest scrap of food!

After they had both finished, Tam lay in his bed and I got into mine. All I could hear was the clattering of plastic trays followed by the stomping of feet. Maia really didn't seem very tired. I gave her some time to explore the spare room before calling her into her bed. She came running in, ears pricked with a manic look on her face. How on earth was I going to convince her that it was bedtime and she had to settle? I switched off the lights hoping that she would get the hint but ooooh no! She grabbed her little teddy and shot back into the other room. I admitted defeat. Maia would come to bed when she was ready.

It wasn't too long before she returned. She had a good long sniff at her bedding before climbing into her bed. She turned three circles, made sure that she had the perfect spot then flopped down into her bed. As with previous nights, she started licking and nibbling at herself. It was a behaviour that I had observed quite a lot during the day but at bedtime it seemed particularly persistent. I have to admit that this was quite distracting as not only was the sound amplified in the darkness, but every time she licked, her jaw clicked with a bone-on-bone crunch. It was horrible! I let Maia have a few minutes of jaw cracking licking until I couldn't stand it any longer. I quietly interrupted Maia by telling her it was bedtime and thankfully she got the hint. She quickly settled down and I didn't hear another peep out of her until the morning.

There could be several possible explanations why Maia did this licking behaviour. She could have some sort of allergy that caused her skin to feel irritated and itchy. There was a lot of pollen around at that time of year. She rarely broke the skin, but she was very persistent and if I didn't interrupt her she would just go on and on.

It was also possible that she might have pain somewhere and was licking to ease the pain or give her a distraction to take her mind off it. She had been holding so much tension in her body for such a long time it would be reasonable to expect that she was holding pain there somewhere. I would have loved to get a chiropractor to look at her but Maia was a long way off letting a stranger do any body work with her. It was also possible that Maia was compelled to lick as she got comfort from it. This behaviour could have developed several years ago, before she was rescued by Forever Hounds Trust as a way to cope with her stress and trauma. Alternatively it may have started while she was in kennels, as licking would have given her something to do while she spent many hours alone. Whatever the cause, it seemed to have become a bit of a compulsion for her. I decided to monitor it and then decide the best way forward. If it was a coping strategy I certainly didn't want to prevent her from doing it but if she was doing it because she was uncomfortable then I would definitely have to intervene. Something to ponder … and something to keep me awake all night over-thinking.

Tam keeping a really close eye on Maia

TWELVE - Day 5

Maia had been settling in really well and our relationship was building. I wanted to try and help her understand that if she got worried about anything, she should always come to me and I would take care of it. This was a huge ask for her as she had a very high sense of self-preservation and had learnt to be totally independent from humans. It would be a huge step to expect her to put her trust in me. My first step was to use her very well-practised flight response to teach her to come with me and follow my lead. I waited until she was at the bottom of the garden, then I called "Maia, let's go" in a really excited voice and then ran into the cottage. I knew that by running back into the house I would trigger Maia's natural chase instinct and she would run with me. When we got into the kitchen I gave her loads of praise. We went back out into the garden and after a while we did it again. Very quickly Maia started to see it as a bit of a game and got really excited when we ran inside. Of course she runs considerably faster than me, so as we ran inside, she began to bounce up and down as she ran alongside me to slow herself down which was very sporting of her!

Maia was learning a really important lesson. The "let's go" cue was something I would rely on a lot when we started to go out on walks. Whenever Maia came across anything she was worried about such as walkers approaching, I could give her the "let's go" cue, quickly get her attention and then about-turn and lead her away from whatever it was that had scared her. She would still move away from whatever was frightening her but it was done in a more controlled way than her 'panic then bolt' tendencies.

The "let's go" game became a full on game in its own right. It still meant 'let's run inside' but I added "and back again" so I would run back down the garden with Maia in hot pursuit. Not only was it a good way of exercising her as it often descended into zoomies, but we had found a way to play chase together despite the obvious human versus sight hound limitations! It was a great example of where learning can take place through play outside a training session. Maia was learning without even realising she was learning.

There was just one slight obstacle to our game - Tam! Maia wasn't the only one learning the new cues. Tam was also very keen to join in. This did cause one or two significant health and safety concerns. Maia is very agile and light on her feet and is quick to jump out the way if need be. Tam is rather less so. In the middle of our game, he

73

often got confused about whether he was coming or going so would start to spin in the middle of the lawn. Unfortunately I often found myself in the spin zone and while trying to run back up the garden with Maia I felt the full force of his whirling bulk. Another problem was that when Tam ran up and down the garden with Maia, he focussed all his attention on her and didn't look where he was going. There really is nothing quite as frightening as seeing a 36kg golden blur hurtling directly towards you but knowing it hasn't even seen you. Whatever - or whoever - was in Tam's flight path ran a very real risk of being mown down.

Barb's visit had gone so well that I felt Maia was ready to meet some-one new. My friend Sue was keen to meet her and as an experienced Healing Practitioner I knew that whenever Maia got anxious, Sue would be able to send her some healing to help her feel safe and calm again. If Maia accepted Sue, I also hoped it would give me the opportunity to take Tam out for a quick run which he desperately needed. Sue kindly offered to pick up some groceries for me which was a real help as my chicken reserves were running low. The shops were just a few minutes away but I didn't feel that Tam and Maia were ready to be left alone just yet.

In preparation for our visitor, I needed to have a quick vacuum. I had put this off as long as possible as many dogs are scared of the noise and vibrations of vacuum cleaners. Even Tam, who'd been carefully introduced to the vacuum since he was a puppy, still preferred to leave the room when it was running. I wasn't sure how Maia would react so I watched her very closely as I got the cleaner out. To my surprise she didn't react at all. I carefully unravelled the cable - still nothing. I braced myself, took a deep breath and prepared myself for a Maia meltdown as I switched on the vacuum cleaner. Then ... nothing! No reaction from her *at all*. She didn't even lift her head from her slumber on the sofa. Clearly vacuum cleaners weren't an issue for Maia. One thing we could check off the scary list.

It was really important that when Sue arrived she behaved exactly as Barb had—just come in, sit in the same seat and completely ignore Maia. Keeping everything very consistent and predictable would really help to build Maia's confidence. In time, I hoped she would realise that visitors were nothing to fear as all they did was come in and ignore her.

After a phone briefing and extensive instructions Sue arrived right on time. I asked her to leave the shopping in the car so she didn't come in carrying lots of rustling carrier bags, which could frighten Maia.

Tam gave Sue a fabulous welcome. It was several minutes before she could get past security and quietly take her seat on the sofa. Maia took up position in her den and watched Sue very closely over the arm of the sofa. I don't think she could quite believe that I had the audacity to invite someone else round and let them sit on her sofa. Again! Tam did a great job entertaining Sue and diverted all attention away from Maia. He hadn't seen Sue for some time and he had a lot of catching up to do.

After the commotion had died down a bit I went into the kitchen to make us a cup of tea. I could see that Maia was having the same quandary she had experienced with Barb. She really wanted to get on the sofa but wasn't quite brave enough. I returned to the living room and sat on the floor opposite the sofa. Within seconds I had 36kg of overexcited golden retriever sitting on my lap. He might be huge but Tam had never lost the belief that he was a lap-dog.

After a few minutes of chat, Maia could stand it no more and climbed onto the sofa and lay in a tense ball in the furthest corner from Sue. We weren't expecting that! Maia behaved just as she had when she first joined me on the sofa, grasping on to every tiny thread of confidence she could muster. We were both holding our breath and trying to stay calm but it was a wonderful moment.

It was time to show Maia that strangers can bring tasty benefits. I put a large handful of diced chicken in a bowl and then put it on a little table beside Sue. I took a piece, gave it to Maia and then sat back down on the floor. Maia could smell the chicken in the air and it had certainly sparked her interest. After a while I asked Sue to get a piece of chicken and without looking at Maia, put it down on the sofa in front of where she was lying. Maia tensed up and was ready to jump off the sofa as Sue's hand approached her. She watched very suspiciously as the chicken was placed in front of her and then looked a little surprised when Sue moved her hand away without making any attempt to stroke her. This wasn't what Maia was expecting at all. After a few seconds she ate the chicken.

Sue offered Maia another piece and this time she took it a little more confidently. Resisting the temptation to look at, or talk to Maia, Sue continued to give her small pieces of chicken. I could see that Maia was thinking about what was happening. Perhaps strangers = chicken? After a while she seemed quite settled around Sue so I felt that we could ask a little more from Maia in order to earn her chicken reward. Following my direction, Sue offered Maia small pieces of chicken to be taken from her hand. As before, Sue avoided looking at Maia or talking to her. After brief hesitation Maia's inexhaustible appetite for chicken took over and she reached round and tentatively took the chicken from Sue's hand.

Several hours passed and Maia and Sue's relationship seemed to be blossoming, so I felt we were ready to take the next step. When Sue went to give Maia a piece of chicken I asked her to give Maia a little stroke on her shoulder with the back of her hand and then immediately give Maia the reward. Sue slowly reached across to Maia and gave her a really gentle stroke. Maia jumped as Sue touched her but she didn't try to move away. She then eagerly took the chicken and looked up at Sue asking for more. This was such a huge step for Maia - accepting the touch from a stranger albeit one who was laden with chicken! We repeated it several times. The only time she looked unsettled was when Sue glanced across at her as she stroked her. Maia immediately turned away, started fidgeting and looked very uncomfortable. She was starting to accept touch which was amazing but even brief eye contact was still way too much. Thankfully there was no lasting harm done to Maia's confidence and she continued to accept Sue's touch as long as she did so without looking at her.

Another hour or so passed and Maia seemed really comfortable with Sue. She didn't even seem to worry when I went out to the garden for a game with Tam which was amazing. If she could cope while we were in the garden, perhaps she could cope if I took Tam out for a run in the field. The wonders of modern technology meant that I could stay on the phone to Sue the whole time and I knew I could be back home within minutes. For Tam's sake it was worth a try.

So, what was the best way of doing this? I knew that Tam would be really excited - and very noisy - if he knew he was going for a walk which could unsettle Maia. After considering all the options, I had a plan. First I would distract Tam by throwing his favourite toy into the back garden. Then, I would quietly collect his harness and lead which were hanging by the back door and take them out into the garden. Then I could tack him up outside and we could slip out through the garden gate, through the copse and into the fields. That was the plan. Unfortunately I greatly underestimated Tam's ability to know what I was thinking. The moment I went to get up, he knew! He went from fast asleep to rampaging bull in an instant, play bowing, spinning, barking and jumping up and down on the spot. Unsurprisingly, Maia took fright at the commotion, leapt off the sofa and ran into her den.. Time for plan B - except I didn't have a plan B! The damage was done. Sue had been feeding Maia tiny pieces of chicken and sending healing for several hours now and I felt that their relationship was reasonably secure. Rather than trying to calm Tam down and have another go later, I felt it would be best for us just to go. I grabbed his harness and lead on the way and closed the door behind me.

Tam was thrilled to be going out. As I put his harness on my mind was racing. What was Maia doing now? Has she returned to the sofa or was she still hiding in her den? Perhaps she was frantically running around the cottage in a panic fretting that we had gone. What if this caused her to relapse after she had been doing so well? Arrgh, there were so many questions running through my head. Before I had even made it down to the bottom of the garden I called Sue from my mobile to check. To my great relief she told me that Maia had already jumped back on the sofa and had been nudging her for chicken. It was way better than I could have hoped. As Tam and I set off through the copse I received a running commentary. Maia was on the sofa training Sue in the art of rapid-fire chicken delivery and was proving to be a very demanding teacher!

Tam was so happy to be out. It was lovely to see him bounding across the field, tail up, ears flapping, golden locks flowing in the breeze. For a short time he didn't have a care in the world. It had been such a confusing time for him since Maia arrived. He had made so many sacrifices but wasn't really enjoying many benefits. This walk was so important for him to shed some tension and let off some steam. Sue reported that all was still going well. Maia seemed settled and relaxed. There was only one problem. Sue had been a little too generous with the chicken and the supply was starting to get low. Tight rationing would be required to make the remaining chicken last until we got back.

I decided to carry on across the next field. It was such a beautiful afternoon and Tam and I were having such a lovely time - it was just like the old days. As I was striding through the grass I had a reality check. Maia was the most amazing addition to our family but our lives would never be the same again. It was going to be a long time before Maia would be able to join us on our walks and almost unimaginable to think that one day she might run free across the field with Tam. As we got to the stile, Tam was keen to carry on along the footpath but I felt I that we really should get back to Sue and Maia. It was with some sadness that I turned back as we were having such a lovely walk and I wasn't sure when we would be able to get out again. Another quick update from Sue confirmed that rationing had done the trick and there were still a few scraps of chicken that would keep Maia satisfied until we returned - as long as we weren't too long!

We arrived back home and Tam got a fantastic welcome from Maia. She leapt off the sofa and rushed up to him, poking her pointy nose right in his face. Tam raised his head to try and avoid the pokes and then went to Sue for some attention and sympathy. Time for a cup of tea and a thorough debrief. I wanted to know EVERYTHING - every tiny thing that Maia had done, every detail, every nuance. As Sue started to recall Maia's behaviour, it was clear that Maia hadn't really missed us at all. It was a huge relief. All in all it had been really encouraging. It was confirmation that I had a system in place that enabled Maia to feel safe around - carefully selected - visitors.

Before we knew it, the afternoon had flown by and it was time for Sue to leave. As she got up Maia immediately jumped off the sofa and looked very worried. Her reaction was perfectly understandable. She had been quite settled when Sue was seated but Sue was much more intimidating when she was standing up - all 158cms of her! Despite sitting next to Sue for several hours and munching her way through several cooked chicken breasts, it still wasn't enough to ease Maia's mistrust. I asked Sue to avoid interacting with Maia and walk away. As soon as she did Maia returned to her seat on the sofa.

Maia had done so well, I would stick to our protocol with visitors until Maia was completely confident. When visitors were seated they were very predictable but as soon as they stood up she was worried about what they might do to her. She was a complicated little hound and there was never going to be a quick fix.

After Sue left I took the dogs out into the garden. Maia had been on the sofa for hours so it was time she had a good leg stretch. It would also help her let go of any tension left over from Sue's visit. After a wee and a sniff round, Maia did a lovely play bow to Tam and then took off round the garden at break-neck speed. Tam was still a bit excited from Sue's visit so quickly set off in hot pursuit. His intention was definitely friendly but as Maia saw him drawing closer she took fright, yelped and ran back inside. Noooo! Tam was trying so hard to join in but again Maia seemed really intimidated by him. I called Tam over and gave him loads of praise as he hadn't done anything wrong. Maia just needed more time. It was more than clear by now that her first love was food, closely followed by her need for comfort. Perhaps I could use these to help bring Tam and Maia together...

The dogs had come to a bit of a stalemate. Tam would approach Maia, give her a sniff and then do a lovely polite play bow, only for Maia to look away and completely snub him. They were both such playful dogs but they couldn't work out how to play *together*. I had to find a way to get Maia off the sofa so they could spend some quality time together and perhaps even strike up a game - the problem was that if it was a choice between the comfy sofa or the floor, Maia was going to choose the sofa every time. I didn't want to restrict her access to the sofa as it had become her safe place. I needed to come up with something that would give Maia a comfortable alternative to the sofa that would also be accessible to Tam.

After having a rummage through my cupboards I found a spare double duvet. I folded it in half then lay it on the floor in the middle of my living room. It didn't take long for Tam to go and investigate. Tam was first to test the duvet for comfort and lay down right across the middle. It definitely looked like it passed the comfort test and met with his approval. Then a little more tentatively Maia went to investigate. After giving the duvet a thorough sniff, she lay down on the edge of the duvet next to Tam. Result! Stage 1 of operation friendship was complete. There was definitely a bit of tension but absolutely no animosity between them. I gave them both loads of praise to reassure them that they were doing a good job but it was all a bit awkward. They needed something to do together. Then I had the idea to give them each an identical toy bone to chew. I knew that there would be no competition over them as Maia was so submissive and Tam was not at all possessive. It worked a treat. They both started intently chomping on their bones. Perfect. It was great to see them sharing the same space together without the awkwardness of what to do next.

There was something quite amusing and fascinating as I watched Maia trying to chew her bone. It seemed that she didn't really know how to hold it in order to chew it. Where most dogs would hold a bone in between their paws, with the bone pointing upwards for them to chew, Maia stretched and contorted her long neck so that she could chew her bone while it was lying flat on the floor. Then she tried to hold it between her knees - she really was not making life easy for herself. It was very odd! Whatever her technique, the bone chewing distraction certainly did the trick. As they were chewing Maia was slowly edging her way closer to Tam until they were lying side by side and almost touching. It was so lovely to see. The bones enabled the dogs to learn to be next to each other in a non-confrontational way. After about ten minutes, Maia stopped chewing her bone and Tam reached across and took it for himself.

As he did so, Maia took his bone and started chewing that in her own unique style. They both seemed completely at ease.

Eventually, Maia finished chewing and made a very bold decision. She tentatively rolled on to her side so that she was making physical contact with Tam. It was wonderful to see Maia trying to snuggle with Tam but sadly it didn't quite go according to plan. Tam was taken quite by surprise. He really didn't know how to take it. I tried to reassure him but he clearly felt uncomfortable and got up and walked away. Aaarrgh! So near but yet so far, it was such a shame. Maia had attempted such a lovely gesture but had been rebuked. Even though we didn't have the fairy tale ending, Tam and Maia had definitely laid the foundations in their budding friendship.

Later that evening, it was time to let the dogs out for their last toilet before bedtime. They both did what they had to do and then all of a sudden I experienced one of the most terrifying and wonderful experiences of my life. Night-time zoomies! This is when Maia runs round the garden at top speed but this time it was in the pitch dark. Despite his disappointment earlier that day when Maia stopped zoomies as soon as he joined in, Tam was quick to give chase. I could hear the thundering of lurcher and golden retriever paws as they stampeded around the garden - and the thwack of leaves as they skimmed past the shrubs - but I could barely see them. It is scary enough watching zoomies in broad daylight, but at night time it takes on a different vibe! Then, just as quickly as it started Maia raced back into the house. Game over.

THIRTEEN - Day 6

It was another beautiful day. Maia seemed to be finding her feet and Tam started to relax a little more around her instead of keeping a constant nervous eye on her. We were all starting to get into a routine and the bubbling tension between Tam and Maia seemed to ease a little.

After rejecting her breakfast yet again it was starting to concern me that Maia didn't really seem to have much of an appetite. She was still receiving quite a lot of her daily ration in the form of food rewards during training and I deducted that amount from her total daily ration to ensure I wasn't over-feeding her. However, it was essential that she ate her kibble to ensure she ate a balanced diet. She seemed to get excited as I prepared her food and was keen to tuck in when I put it down for her but after eating all the wet meat, she just picked at the kibble. I remembered seeing quite a lot of food in her bowl when I visited her in kennels which made me think that perhaps she didn't have much interest in food, but having lived with her for nearly a week, I knew that wasn't the case. Maia LOVED food. Then I had that sinking feeling, perhaps she just didn't like *this* food. When I asked what food Maia was being fed, perhaps I should also have checked that she actually liked it!

I feel it is really important that dogs have food that they enjoy. Eat food you don't like or go hungry doesn't seem like much of a choice to me. I feel it is our responsibility to find something they really do like. Maia continued to pick at her food but didn't eat much and judging from the amount of kibble left in her bowl it certainly seemed like she didn't really enjoy it. I had to find an acceptable alternative so I decided to give her a few pieces of Tam's kibble just to see what she made of it. Tam's kibble was approximately £25 a bag more expensive than Maia's so I was a little hesitant. With some reluctance I mixed some of Tam's kibble in with Maia's, added a little wet meat and gave it back to her. As she had done before, she ate the wet meat and then started picking at the kibble.

As she was eating I started to consider other possible reasons that might dissuade her from tucking into the kibble. Perhaps she had pain in her mouth or problems with her teeth that made eating dry food uncomfortable? It was possible but she had received a check up from Forever Hounds Trust's vet just days before she came to me and they didn't spot anything concerning. I didn't really want to take a look in Maia's mouth if I could avoid it as it is such an invasive thing to do and I didn't feel that our relationship was secure enough yet. Perhaps she had neck or back pain? Again, nothing was detected during her pre-homing vet check. I would of course take her to my vet to be checked out if she needed it but I didn't want to put her through the stress of a vet visit unless absolutely necessary.

After a minute or so Maia walked away from her bowl. It came as no surprise that she had left most of the kibble. But hang on, on closer inspection I saw that she had eaten all of Tam's kibble and left her own. She must have taken each piece, rolled it around her mouth before deciding whether she would eat it or reject it! I gave her a small handful of Tam's kibble and she couldn't eat it fast enough. Oh dear, it really seemed like she didn't have an issue with kibble, she just didn't like *her* kibble. So that was that. Trust me to take on a kennel hound with expensive taste. From that day on, Maia feasted on Tam's kibble and our local rescue centre was the lucky beneficiary of a 12kg bag of kibble - minus a few very expensive handfuls!

One of Maia's issues was that she toileted in the home. It is such a common problem but one that can usually be resolved with a lot of commitment and many, many hours stood out in the garden in all weathers saying 'wee-wees' repeatedly! It was difficult to know whether Maia had ever been house trained and forgotten or whether she had never been properly trained. Certainly for a young dog spending so many months in a kennel, she could be forgiven for getting out of the routine of toileting outside. There was also a strong possibility that Maia's toileting issues could be related to her over-whelming anxiety.

I decided to start from the very beginning. I had to convince this scaredy rain-averse lazy hound that toileting outside was actually a really good thing to do. This could be tricky. Why on earth would Maia want to go all the way outside to my scary garden, come rain or shine, just to toilet when she could do it in the comfort and safety of the cottage? She might take quite a lot of convincing!

I had to make it clear what I was asking and make it really worth her while if she made the effort to do as I asked. Consistency was key. I would try and ensure that Maia had every opportunity to toilet out-side. When she did I had to go over the top with praise and give her a fabulous food reward so that she would be motivated to do it again.

First I identified the times when Maia was more likely to need to go out. They were first thing in the morning, after meals, immediately after I got home and last thing at night. At these times I would go out in the garden with Maia and wait for her to empty. Sometimes it would happen quickly after which the celebrations could begin and we could all get back inside. At other times I would be standing out in the garden for ages waiting for her, much to the amusement and bemusement of my not particularly dog-loving neighbours. It became a friendly battle of wills, one that I hoped to win before the colder, wetter weather kicked in.

At the beginning I watched Maia almost continually. If she showed signs of wanting to toilet such as getting off the sofa, sniffing around the floor or circling, I could jump in, distract her and take her outside. There were a few occasions when I couldn't watch her. One situation that proved to be vulnerable to accidents was, rather strangely, when I was in the shower. On one occasion after breakfast the dogs were resting in the living room after their garden romp. I assumed Maia had toileted. BIG mistake! I took a quick shower, got dressed and then went into the living room. The dogs hadn't moved at all - or so it seemed. As I stood on the rug and looked across to Maia I felt warmth seeping up through my newly laundered socks. You guessed it. She had done a wee in the living room and I was standing right in it. Yuck! I didn't tell Maia off as it was my fault I had given her the opportunity to make a mistake. I was disappointed and angry at myself. Maia had had no accidents up to that point. I rolled up the rug and put it in the washing machine. I just hoped that now she had toileted in the cottage once, Maia wouldn't make a habit of it. Frustratingly it wasn't a one off.

We went through a five day period when whatever time of the day I showered I would come out to a wee on the living room floor. The only way to break this pattern was to take my shower as soon as Maia had been in the garden and emptied. Now it's not ideal to have your shower time dictated to you by your dog but I knew that it was a short-term inconvenience for long-term gain. It worked. One week passed with no accidents. When I reverted to showering to my own schedule, the problem of Maia weeing while I had a shower never recurred.

Another occasion, in week two at about 4pm, Maia took to weeing in the living room, even if she had just been out in the garden. It continued for several days and sometimes she even did it right in front of me which suggested that she really didn't know what she was doing was 'wrong'. When I caught her in the act, I called her outside and gave her the 'wee-wees' cue and lots of praise. Maia was still quite fearful of the garden but it was clear that she was really trying to do as I asked. Luckily she got the idea reasonably quickly. The only other time we had an issue was when I had just started leaving Tam and Maia home alone. I took them into the garden before I went out and waited for ages so that Maia had every opportunity to toilet. Did she? No. She just stood next to me, looking up at me with the sweetest expression and did nothing. I was only gone for about 15 minutes, but when I returned I found a puddle on the rug on the living room floor. I deliberately didn't take any notice of the puddle as I didn't want to make a big issue of it. Maia hadn't toileted to be naughty, there would be a good reason and it was up to me to work out what it was.

I played back the video to find out what had happened when I went out. Less than two minutes after I left, Maia did the wee. So it seemed possible that anxiety played a part in her toileting issues; uncertainty of my departure or perhaps she was slightly intimidated by Tam when I wasn't around? It gave me a lot to think about. What I saw next on the video absolutely crushed me. I saw Tam walk up to where Maia had toileted and try to hide it. He pushed at the rug with his nose again and again until eventually he had managed to flip the corner over on itself so Maia's puddle was no longer visible. Tam had never toileted in the cottage except when his allergies caught up with him. If he did have an accident, he always covered it over with whatever he could find - often ending up with carpet burns on his nose after pushing rugs, towels or vetbeds the length of the cottage. I have never told him off for having accidents. I found it devastating that he was so worried about Maia's accident that he felt he needed to act. I had to get on top of this toileting issue not just for me and Maia but also for Tam's sake.

Strangely, that was the only time Maia toileted in the cottage when I went out and to this day I am not sure why. At least Tam would never find himself in that situation again.

It took about three weeks for us to crack the toilet training and Maia hasn't had an accident since. Once she has learnt something she rarely forgets. Even now, nearly one year on, I give her loads of praise when she comes in from the garden after emptying. Her training was such a positive experience for her that she is still really pleased with herself when she toilets outside. She comes hurtling in to me, tail wagging, a huge grin on her face and then does a couple of spins. That's what positive reward-based training is all about!

FOURTEEN - Day 7

I had been sitting on the grass in the garden listening to the birds singing and soaking up the beautiful sunshine when my thoughts were rudely interrupted by the thundering of lurcher feet. As my awareness was sharply brought back into focus, I looked up to see Maia charging towards me like a torpedo. I didn't have much time to think but I certainly remember thinking "I hope she has seen me". In a flash she skimmed past me, narrowly missing Tam, skidded round the apple tree then careered back up the garden. She momentarily disappeared from view as she dived behind shrubs then emerged half way down the garden in full flight, directly towards me again. As she flew past, Tam decided to join in the chase. He tried running after her but quickly realised that he was woefully slow. Instead, he decided to cut her off when she re-emerged from behind the shrubs. Unfortunately Maia wasn't expecting to see Tam lolloping along and blocking her route. She tried to swerve but was travelling way to fast and the inevitable happened. Maia ran straight into him! Now Maia might be a skinny, bony lurcher but Tam is a very well-padded chap. Not only does he have an incredibly thick coat, he has loads of loose skin that wobbles as he walks. Luckily these two features combined to help cushion the impact thus preventing serious injury. Maia took off back into the cottage and Tam was left standing in the middle of the garden looking somewhat bewildered. It was almost as if he didn't know what had hit him! I went to check on Maia with a sense of foreboding. She was up on the sofa panting hard and trying to catch her breath after her exertions. I called her off the sofa and with my heart in my mouth checked that all her legs were in the right place, checked that nothing was sticking out where it shouldn't be and checked her all over for cuts. Thankfully she seemed OK. It looked like she had dodged a bullet. Or maybe Tam had.

The garden lent itself to a figure of eight circuit. Out the passageway, down to the far end of the garden, round the apple tree, back up the garden then sharp bend to the left behind the shrubs and through the flowerbed back on the lawn and down round the tree again. The sprint was approximately 20 metres but the bends at either end were quite tight and came up fast. Maia was still finding her feet and her balance so the corners were coming up rather too quickly for her. These two were going to have to work out their zoomies routes to avoid future crashes. Unfortunately Maia's desire for speed was way ahead of her spatial awareness and coordination. This little speed demon was going to have to be a bit more careful.

Despite the heart-in-mouth moment it had been lovely seeing Maia so playful and Tam doing his best to join in the game. They still had so much to learn about each other and they were trying, which was fantastic. When we returned to the garden it seemed that the crash hadn't had a negative 'impact' on their friendship. They set off to investigate the garden together, stopping to sniff if anything caught their attention as they went. What touched me most was that as they walked down the garden side by side, both tails were wagging. It was such a beautiful sight. I could almost hear Handel's Halleluiah chorus ringing in my ears. It was such a breakthrough. I just hoped it would continue. When they returned to the cottage, Maia settled in her usual spot and dozed off and peace descended on the cottage. Now I could catch up on some paperwork.

While I was working I saw Tam go up to Maia and give her a good sniff all over. He started with her tail, then moved on to her paws and legs, tummy and finally her face. When she was awake Tam was not really sure what to make of her, but now she was asleep he could have a really good look. I kept a close eye on him during his fact-finding mission as I didn't want him to wake Maia and startle her, but this encounter had given him a good opportunity to learn more about her without being poked in the face. Then Tam took himself back to his bed to process what he had learnt. It was clearly quite exhausting as before long Tam was fast asleep, snoring quietly. Back to work ...

My peace was short lived. It wasn't long before Tam woke and was bored and whingy. He always starts off whining very quietly under his breath but if he doesn't get any attention he quickly ramps up the volume to a full blown and rather deafening 'woof!' The combination of big brother responsibilities and a lack of exercise were taking its toll. Tam needed some fun. Luckily I had a treat in store for him later that afternoon as I was expecting a delivery of his food which always comes in large cardboard boxes. Tam *loves* delivery day, as once I have unpacked his food, he gets to destroy the boxes.

The delivery arrived on time. I took the bags of food out of the box and threw the empty box onto the living room floor. Tam did what could best be described as a Superman impression as he threw himself onto the box. With that, Maia leapt off the sofa, did two high speed laps of the living room, fled from the room through the kitchen, toileting herself as she went and ended up cowering in the bathroom. Oh dear. I guess Maia was not a fan of cardboard boxes then! I went to reassure her but she was absolutely terrified. I had to get the box out of the living room to give her any chance of calming down. Tam would have been devastated if I had taken the box away. After all it had only just arrived and he was so excited with it. The best option was to throw the box out in the garden. Tam seemed quite happy with this arrangement and after eagerly following me out to the garden with said box he continued to destroy it. Once it was completely flattened he went on to release his pent up frustration by ripping the whole thing into tiny pieces. Cardboard therapy.

After Tam and the box had relocated to the garden, Maia nervously ventured back into the living room and onto the sofa. I sat with her for a while to reassure her and she started to calm down which was more than could be said for Tam. Our peace kept being interrupted by excited barking coming from the garden followed by the sound of tearing cardboard. Tam had definitely needed that. The only negative was that I spent the rest of the evening, crawling around the garden on my hands and knees picking up tiny pieces of shredded cardboard that had blown into the shrubs. It was worth it though. Tam was now a very happy and content chap and I knew that I would have a nice peaceful evening.

As I started to spend more time with Maia there were a few issues that were causing concern. I started to question whether she might have a problem with her eyesight as her spatial awareness seemed a bit amiss. She didn't seem to judge distance well and I noticed that she would often trip over rugs or toys even when they were right in front of her. It was hard to know whether her eyesight was compromised in some way or whether she was too busy focussing on other things - such as what Tam and I were doing - to notice what was in front of her. I did wonder if her issues could also be due to spending such a long time in an empty kennel where she didn't have to worry about tripping over anything. Perhaps she had just got out of the habit of looking where she was going. But then she was pretty bad at catching flies too even if they were right in front of her. It was like she saw them from a distance but couldn't see them when she was up close. An issue with her eyesight could also help explain why she was so anxious and hyper-alert. If she couldn't rely on her eyesight to get information about her environ-ment she might be relying more on the other senses to compensate. That could explain why she was so sensitive to touch, sound and particularly smell, which was a bit odd considering she was a sight hound. If Maia's sight wasn't very good it could also contribute to her great fear of strangers. If she could see people   approach but couldn't see them very well as they got closer, it could be very frightening. As was becoming the norm with Maia, there were so many questions and no answers. If it continued to be an issue I would take her to the vets to get her checked out, but as it wasn't urgent I felt it could wait. A visit to the vet at this stage would be very stressful for Maia and could knock the very fragile confidence and trust she was building. I decided to monitor her closely and continue to build her confidence. That way if she did need any further investigations down the line, she would be much better equipped to cope with them.

Tam in cardboard heaven

FIFTEEN ~ Week 2

Week two and Maia was starting to find her feet. She was getting more confident in the cottage and was hardly using the den at all. Instead she had chosen the sofa to be her safe place. I didn't want to take the den away yet in case she ever needed to use it in the future but it did seem like it was being rather under-used.

Spotting an opportunity, Tam began to use the den in the evenings. As Maia fell asleep on the sofa, Tam would quietly take his place in the den. Comfort always came way down the list of Tam's priorities so that wasn't the draw. No, Tam was drawn to the den because if it was good enough for Maia it was good enough for him! When I walked past him in the evening he looked so peaceful and content. Mind you, the den is right next to the Adaptil diffuser so it's not surprising he looked so chilled. It was lovely that what was originally intended for Maia was now being time-shared very amicably between the two of them. I guess that meant it would be staying then!

By the end of the first week I was starting to understand Maia a bit more. After all that time in kennels, it turned out that Maia was actually a bit of a telly addict. She lay on the sofa watching TV for hours on end. I had to be a bit careful about the programmes she watched. Her favourites were wildlife programmes. She clearly had very good taste in broadcasters as Sir David Attenborough seemed to be a particular favourite. Those calm, relaxing tones combined with images of small furry creatures was a definite winner. However, when it came to dog programmes I had to be careful. Maia was fascinated by watching pictures of dogs, but if she heard any barking she seemed to get very worried very quickly. This was particularly notable in dog rescue scenes. On hearing dogs barking in a kennel environment she leapt off the sofa and paced round the living room with her tail between her legs looking very worried. Perhaps distressed dogs barking was a trigger that took her back to less happy times? I clearly had to try and avoid watching those programmes, or only watch them with the volume down and subtitles on, until Maia was more settled.

I also noticed that while watching TV Maia became uneasy if the presenters were whistling or humming. I can understand whistling as dogs pick up on higher frequency sounds than humans. Although it didn't seem to bother Tam at all. The humming was more of a mystery. Perhaps someone from her past used to hum when they were around her. Whatever the reason, Maia's reaction suggested that she was very uneasy about it.

I was starting to build a good picture of Maia's fear triggers. Her reaction to cardboard boxes had been really extreme and it seemed that barking dogs, people talking, humming or whistling on TV, the sight or sound of people in the garden and going out in the rain were all things we were going to have to work on. The list was getting longer and then there were the carrier bags ...

The sound of rustling plastic bags was another significant trigger for Maia. As soon as she heard even the quietest of rustles, she was off the sofa and into the bathroom in a real panic. I wondered if she'd had a bad experience with a carrier bag - perhaps she had got tangled up in one or had something thrown at her that was inside a carrier bag. Either way, that sound resulted in an extreme panic response.

This was something I needed to address. I had to teach her that the sound of rustling plastic was nothing to be afraid of and actually could be a great sound as it signalled the arrival of chicken.

I built up Maia's exposure to the rustle slowly and carefully. The aim was to get her used to the sound at a very low level. Once she could cope with that I could gradually build up the volume and length of time of the rustle. If done correctly I could slowly increase her tolerance to the noise.

At first I made sure that I was as far away from Maia as possible before giving a sandwich bag in my pocket a quick and barely discernible rustle. Maia heard it immediately. She pricked her ears but held her nerve and didn't leap off the sofa. Great, that was exactly what I wanted. I immediately praised her and gave her a small piece of chicken. Maia was still learning the concept of being rewarded for a target behaviour and hadn't yet made the connection between tolerating something unpleasant and earning a reward. With her insatiable appetite for chicken, I had no doubt that before long she would start to understand.

I repeated the very quiet rustle and reward exercise a few more times until Maia was barely responding to the sound. She had coped really well so I felt that she had done enough for one session.

I built up Maia's exposure to the noise of rustling plastic bags very gradually over the coming months until she had completely over-come her fear. It took a while but it was worth it. By the end of her training Maia didn't show any reaction at all even if she heard big carrier bags or bin-liners rustling right in front of her. Mind you, her training had been a little bit too successful as by the time we had finished she wouldn't think twice about poking her nose into my carrier bags as soon as I return from a shopping trip. Once I had just returned from the pet shop with lots of goodies in a plastic carrier bag. I put it down on the floor for barely 30 seconds when I heard a sharp tugging on the bag. Maia had found a bag of treats inside and was having a tug of war with the carrier bag in an attempt to steal the treats! Perhaps I am being unfair. Perhaps Maia wasn't stealing treats from the bag at all. Perhaps she was doing a little refresher course in desensitisation to carrier bags ... hmm, I think not!

Another thing I had to get Maia used to, was being left at home without me. It was great that I'd had the luxury of taking so much time off work to help Maia settle in, but I didn't want her to get too used to having me around all day. I had to prepare her - and remind Tam - so it didn't come as too much of a shock when I went back to work. I didn't anticipate that this would be too much of an issue for Maia as she had spent so much time alone in kennels. Also, I knew I was still far less important to Maia than Tam when it came to keeping company so I didn't feel that she would really miss me that much. Tam would be a different matter.

I wanted to build up the time I was away very gradually. I would leave them for just a few minutes at first and slowly increase the amount of time I was away. The dogs would start to get used to me not being there, without being left so long that they began to worry. When I went out I left them with a snuffle mat each so they had something to do while I was away. Snuffle mats are interactive dog toys that consist of fleece strips tied at one end to a rubber mat base. The other end is left loose. You can then drop kibble on to the mat and dogs use their noses to rummage through the strips and sniff out the kibble. I only gave the dogs the snuffle mats when I went out so it made the mats extra special. Far from worrying about me leaving, Tam and Maia started to look forward to me going out as it signalled that they were about to get something fun and tasty.

In order to see what they got up to when I wasn't there, I set up a camera in the living room. It was fascinating to see how they behaved when I went out. It can be really interesting and often quite surprising to see what our furry friends get up to when they think they are alone.

On the first occasion, I just went and sat in my car for a couple of minutes and then returned. When I replayed the footage I was in for a surprise. After eating all the kibble from her snuffle mat Maia spent the entire time wandering around the cottage sniffing and examining every nook and cranny. Even though we were developing a lovely relationship, it was clear that Maia still felt inhibited when I was at home with her. The footage certainly did expose her curious side. Tam's behaviour was much more concerning. He lay down, head on his paws and watched everything Maia did with a worried look on his face. I felt terrible. This could be a real problem.

I waited for a couple of hours before leaving the cottage again. This time I went out for five minutes. On my return I got a lovely welcome from both dogs. I gave them some praise and then played the footage. Maia continued her exploration - sniffing every corner, poking her nose into the log basket and under the sofa. Then after about three minutes she climbed up on to the sofa and fell asleep. Unfortunately, Tam's behaviour was the same as before. He lay in the same spot and didn't take his eyes off Maia during the whole time I was gone, poor lad. I had brought a new dog into our home as I really wanted a lovely friend and companion for Tam but far from being a comfort, Maia was *adding* to his stress. The dogs were still learning how to get along with each other and without me for backup it looked like Tam was feeling the strain.

I continued to gradually build up the time the dogs were left alone and I monitored Tam's reaction closely from the camera footage when I got home. I felt so guilty. I have always strived to do the best for my dogs and yet I had turned Tam's life upside down. It would be really sad if I had to separate them when I went out. Perhaps Tam just needed a little more time to get used to it. I really hoped so ...

I had been putting off mowing my lawn as Maia was still quite fearful in the garden, but my garden was starting to resemble a hay field just before harvesting. Many dogs have a fear of lawnmowers which isn't really surprising considering the noise, the grass being blasted through the cracks of the collection box, the vibration and the smell. I was mindful that if Maia was in the garden when I mowed the lawn it might add to her general anxiety in the garden and I didn't want to dent her still shaky confidence. As a precaution I shut Tam and Maia in the kitchen, set up the extension lead and got the lawnmower from the shed. I started to mow the lawn and apart from my poor mower struggling to get through the very long grass, all was going well. I made my way down the garden and needed to release a bit more cable from the extension lead. As I turned round I nearly tripped over Maia! I am not sure when she got out or how long she had been following me around the garden, but one thing was clear, Maia didn't have a problem with lawnmowers! She continued to follow me around while I finished mowing the lawn. Like the vacuum cleaner, it seemed that electrical appliances weren't an issue for Maia. She really was a complex yet surprising little hound. To this day I still have no idea how they managed to break out of the kitchen. I can only imagine that I didn't shut the door securely but I am usually very careful. I guess it will remain another of life's little mysteries.

I noticed on a few occasions that Maia would start to nibble at her bedding. Judging by the state of the little teddy in her kennel this might be something she did regularly, perhaps for comfort or for entertainment. Either way, it was not something I wanted to continue. When I saw Maia nibbling I gave her a quiet 'a-aa' to distract her and then gave her a toy that she was allowed to nibble. If nibbling soft textiles was something she liked to do, I wanted to give her an alternative that didn't involve sofas, cushions, throws or her own bedding. Maia was easy to distract but I was slightly concerned that if I wasn't there I might come home to a trashed cottage one day. As it turned out Maia learnt very quickly.

I consider myself quite lucky as I only ended up with a couple of throws with one small hole in each and a slightly nibbled trim on a cushion. It could have been far, far worse.

Since Maia arrived I had been giving her frequent healing sessions as we were settled in the evenings. She loved the healing and quickly relaxed into it and the benefit she was gaining from it was clear to see. We had one particularly emotional session where I was sending Maia some healing and I felt a flood of tears pouring down my face. They weren't my tears, they were coming from Maia. When animals release long-held trauma it is not unusual to experience this emotional release. I knew that for Maia, something really significant shifted in that moment. It was another little piece of her past that she could leave behind.

After she woke from her healing her behaviour was really interesting. She looked happy, peaceful and serene almost like a weight had been lifted. She came over and leant into me and then completely melted into my arms. She stayed motionless in that embrace for several minutes and it was another of those moments that I will never forget. I felt so privileged that Maia trusted me enough to let down her barriers and let me get so close to her emotionally. She still had a long way to go but this was a huge test of trust and it seemed that I had passed with flying colours.

SIXTEEN - Week 3

Maia had been with us for just three weeks but it seemed more like three years. She divided her time between playing, investigating, zoomies and recharge, and continued to hugely exceed expectations. Her personality continued to blossom and there were moments where she was absolutely hilarious although poor long-suffering Tam might not always agree. It had become obvious that she was going to be a lazy lurcher. Depending on their breeding, some lurchers can be really hyper and crazy. Not Maia - she is definitely a couch potato kind of a gal! In many ways she was now behaving like a normal well-adjusted dog. It was a clear reminder to never underestimate the incredible power of healing in combination with time and a little bit of behaviour know-how.

We had been spending considerable time just hanging out together in the garden but Maia was still very flighty. She was staying outside for increasing lengths of time with Tam and me, which was great, but on most occasions there would be something that would scare her and she would end up fleeing back inside. There were definite signs that she was making progress but she still had a long way to go before she was relaxed and confident in the garden. With time and positive, rewarding experiences in the garden I felt sure that Maia would over-come her fears.

Another of Maia's fears was fear of men. This was so long-held and extreme that I felt it would be some time before she understood that the men I introduced her to were OK and didn't pose any threat. She needed gradual exposure to kind softly-spoken men, who asked nothing of her to help build her confidence. I knew just the man for the job.

I regularly chatted to John, my neighbour, over the garden gate and Maia often listened in on our conversations from a safe distance. There was an added draw for Maia to eavesdrop as John had a lovely springer spaniel called Riley who usually joined us at the gate during our chats. One afternoon we were having a natter when out of the corner of my eye I saw Maia cautiously approaching. I asked John to completely ignore her and we carried on with our conversation. As we continued to talk, Maia gradually edged closer and closer to us until she was standing right next to me. It was such a bold move from her. She was standing just a few metres away from John, sniffing the air and watching him very closely but she held her ground. It was such a great experience for her as she had the opportunity to watch and learn about John from a position of safety behind the fence. Instead of her usual reaction to flee, it was great to see curiosity kicking in and it was a positive shift in her reaction towards men.

Sadly our progress seemed short-lived as the following day some builders moved into the garden of my other neighbour to do some work on their roof. I was advised they would be there all week and my heart sank - the timing couldn't have been worse. We had been making such great progress in the garden and Maia was starting to get confident enough to stay outside with Tam and me for periods of time before rushing indoors. She was spending less time standing in that hyper-alert mode listening out for any barely discernible noise from which to take fright. I was really concerned that the building work next door could seriously impact her confidence.

We were in the garden on the morning that the builders arrived. One of them said 'hello' and that was enough to cause Maia to panic and flee to the safety of the cottage. In an instant it was like we were back to day one, with Maia trembling and refusing to step foot out in the garden. It was so utterly disappointing and frustrating.

There were three builders, all burly men who spent the day shouting to each other over noisy machinery. They were all very pleasant but they were absolutely terrifying to Maia. I knew this was way too much for her to cope with so I decided to completely avoid taking her into the garden during the day when the builders were there. If I could avoid adding to her fear that week, there was a slim chance that there would be no long term damage to her confidence. We would go out in the garden really early before the builders arrived and then batten down the hatches until they left in the evening. Even when inside the cottage I could see Maia straining to listen out for them so I turned the volume on the television up to the max and prepared myself to endure a week of very noisy daytime television.

I waited for all the builders to leave the site in the afternoon before I turned the television down (bliss!) and attempted to go back out into the garden. I armed myself with a big handful of chicken and made my way outside eagerly accompanied by Tam who'd had a very boring day stuck inside the cottage. I sat down on the grass and prepared myself for a long wait before Maia would emerge.

Tam was delighted to have me all to himself again, throwing his toys around and contorting his body into positions it really wasn't designed for before slamming into me or the ground - whichever was closest! It took about ten minutes for Maia's nose to appear round the corner of the passageway. I saw her sniff the air as she scanned the garden before quickly running back inside. Oh dear, this didn't look good. It was another five minutes before she ventured out again. This time she ran down the garden, stopped and sniffed the air and then ran back indoors again. It was better than her first attempt but it was clear that the builders had shaken her confidence. We would have to go back to the beginning and re-build her confidence.

Maia waited until after dark before she was happy to go into the garden. She stayed outside for quite a while and seemed to be making up for lost time. The peace was broken when I heard the stampede of paws as Maia took off for a silly five minutes round the garden. Tam tried and failed to keep up with her so he tried to block her instead. Maia wasn't going to let a 36kg lump of giddy golden retriever slow her down so she kept up her breakneck speed, ricocheting off the shrubs as she went. I have to admit it was ridiculously funny - like something out of a comedy sketch. I dread to think what damage she had inflicted on my peony as it seemed to bear the brunt of their zoomies fun. I would find out in the morning!

It was with some trepidation that I ventured out into the garden, bright and early the following morning. The sight that greeted me can only be described as complete devastation! My peony was half its original size with broken stems hanging limply, my honesty plants had been flattened and my bedding plants pulverised. All those plants that I had nurtured over the years reduced to nothing more than compostable waste in less than two minutes! I guess there was always next year.

Maia was getting much braver in the garden and more bouncy and playful by the day so I felt it was time to broaden her horizons. I had been waiting for this day with excitement and dread in equal measures. I would have my wingman to give Maia confidence and his bulk might help to keep her straight if she did panic and go to bolt. My over-riding concern was if Maia got spooked on our walk and somehow managed to get away from me. There were always so many heart-breaking posts on social media begging for sightings of dogs that had got frightened and run away. I couldn't imagine how awful it must be to find oneself in that position. I had to ensure that Maia and I stayed attached - no matter what. Following a recommendation from Forever Hounds Trust, I had a martingale collar and a double ended lead in addition to Maia's harness. As lurchers have very narrow sleek heads it is easy for a normal collar to slip over their ears. The martingale is designed to tighten if the lead is pulled tight, to prevent the collar slipping but without restricting them around the neck. One end of the lead would clip to Maia's harness and the other would clip to her collar. I would hold the lead slightly nearer the harness end as my main contact and the end attached to her collar would remain slightly slack. If either failed I had the other for backup.

I collected Tam and Maia's walking kits and started to tack them up. I put Tam's collar and harness on first. He was so delighted that he grabbed a toy and ran into the garden. I wasn't sure how to tell him that Little Sis was coming too! I then called Maia over and started to put her kit on. Despite her excitement she stood really nicely while I put on her collar and fastened her harness. Right, deep breath! I ran through my checklist: Chicken, poo bags, phone, two leads. Everything was ready, it was time to go.

I walked down the garden and met both dogs at the gate. Tam knew exactly where he was going and Maia sensing his excitement, seemed very keen to join him. I clipped on their leads and undid the combination lock on the gate. One last check and we were off!

We crossed my neighbour's garden then walked across a charming but slightly rickety little bridge over the river. The bridge is quite narrow and a bit wobbly but Maia was so eager to keep up with Tam that she didn't seem to notice. We then made our way along a pathway that wound its way through a pretty little copse. We stopped for a moment to catch our breath and take in the scene. The sun was streaming through the trees and the cow parsley looked so green and fresh. It was really beautiful. Tam was sniffing away, busy catching up with all the smells he had missed. Maia stood next to him, head up, tail up and ears pricked, taking it all in. All was well so we continued on through the copse until we got to the stile that marks the entrance to the field. As it was our first trip out, I didn't want to go too far so I decided to turn round and make our way back home. Both dogs were happy to turn back and walked enthusiastically back through the copse, over the bridge and back to our garden gate. All in all, it had gone very well. Both dogs were happy and settled so I felt we could do it again.

As before, we walked over the bridge and up into the copse with both dogs enthusiastically taking the lead. This time things were a little different. Maia knew where she was going this time and pulled like a tank! I was quite taken aback by her strength considering she didn't have much muscle and was still incredibly unfit. She put her head down and really pulled against the lead. While it was great to see her so keen and enthused, this pulling on the lead was something we were going to have to work on. When we got back to the stile I waited for a while to give Maia time to have a good look across the field. I could see her staring across the long grass to the horizon. That would be our destination tomorrow but for today I felt she had gone far enough. Again we turned for home and made our way along the path. It was wonderful seeing the dogs walking side by side so enthusiastically, striding out with their tails wagging in sync.

I stopped as we got to the bridge so that Maia could have a good look at the river below. I didn't want her to suddenly catch sight of it as she was walking over the bridge and frighten herself, but she wasn't the least bit bothered. It was clear that people were her main issue rather than 'things'. We returned to our garden and the dogs waited for me to take their gear off. Maia was panting quite heavily, given we had only been out a few minutes. Mind you, she had been dragging me the entire way! She looked so happy. Her eyes were laughing and she looked so pleased with herself.

Tam's behaviour had been really interesting. Normally he wouldn't have been on the lead and would have been off across the field in a flash. On this walk, he seemed to know that something was different. He accepted that this was just a short walk and made no attempt to continue when I asked him to turn home. Normally he would stop to sniff, trot then stop. This time he kept a nice steady even walking pace which was unusual for him. It was like he knew he had a job to do. Once again he stepped up into the role of big brother and I was so proud of him.

Once we got back to the cottage Tam immediately went to have a drink, swiftly followed by Maia. All in all, our first walk couldn't have gone any better. Another milestone to tick off the list!

The next day, I felt that Maia was ready to go beyond the stile and take a walk in the field. This was a big step as we would be leaving the relative safety of the private copse to join the public footpath across the field. The odds of coming into contact with other walkers and dogs were quite high as it was a popular route.

I live in a small friendly village and have wonderful neighbours. I often met fellow villagers while I was out walking with Tam and it was always great to catch up on village gossip. It also gave me the perfect opportunity to warn them in advance that I would soon be taking in a new dog that was really fearful of people. I explained that if I saw them while I was out with Maia I would be thoroughly anti-social, turn around and walk in the opposite direction - and it was nothing personal! I also asked if they would be kind enough not to let their dogs run over to say 'hello' for a while. Even though Tam would love to play it might be a bit scary for Maia. They were all very understanding and supportive. It was one of the benefits of living in such a lovely small community.

I tacked up the dogs as before and we set off over the bridge and through the copse. Both dogs were delighted to be going out again. This time Maia knew exactly where she was going and pulled hard on the lead. Walking Maia was certainly going to be a full upper body workout for me! We walked briskly to the stile and stopped to survey the field. Sightlines are quite good so I was able to see if anyone was coming from a good 200 metres away.

Now for the challenge of getting two big dogs under a reasonably low stile while I climbed over the top! I had perfected the art with Tam but now I had two leads and two dogs to manoeuvre. Tam went first to show Maia how it was done. She was a little hesitant as she had to work out how to limbo. On her first attempt she didn't get low enough and caught her harness on the bar. That gave her a bit of a fright and caused her to back away. This could be tricky. Tam was one side of the stile waiting enthusiastically to continue his walk and Maia and I were stuck on the other. Luckily Tam stood like a gentleman while Maia regained her composure. After a little reassurance, she made another attempt and success- fully got to the other side. I passed the leads through the stile and climbed over the top and we were off! Walking behind Tam and Maia as they were striding briskly side by side, powering up the slope reminded me of when I used to drive horses, only the horses weren't nearly as strong as these two! It certainly made the climb a little easier than usual. I just hoped that Maia wouldn't be pulling quite so much when we came back down again later.

When we got to the top of the slope Maia froze. Just outside the field about 200 metres away was a layby with two cars parked up. After a few seconds, Maia started to panic. She immediately went into reverse at top speed which was my biggest fear. I was pretty sure she couldn't back out of the harness but I didn't want to find out. I was now being pulled in two directions with Tam walking towards the layby and Maia backing away. I knew that I wouldn't be able to offer Maia much reassurance in this scenario. I needed Tam to help me and that boy was the hero of the moment. He came back and positioned himself by Maia's side. This gave me a second to wrap my arms around her to stop her backing up any further and calm her down. She was trembling throughout her whole body and I could feel her heart pounding. She was so scared. I sent her some healing and it took several minutes before she began to relax. The trembling stopped, her tail came out from between her legs and she started to eat some chicken. Well that had been unexpected! I can only imagine that she either linked the colour or make of the car with one that she had previously had a bad experience with, or she feared that someone would get out of the car. Whatever the reason, the cars were definitely very frightening to her.

I left it up to Maia to decide what we did next. She stood transfixed on the car but didn't seem in any hurry to go back home now. That was fine. We would all just wait and look at the car. Maia needed to watch and understand. She was so quick to react to her fear triggers that she never had the chance to learn that perhaps they weren't quite so frightening after all. She needed time to observe from a safe distance.

After a while Maia was ready to walk again. To my surprise, she chose to make her way back up the slope, in the general direction of the cars! This time I was ready for her. I allowed her to walk a few steps before asking her to wait and then I rewarded her with a little piece of chicken. I didn't want her to walk too far, find herself too close to the cars and take fright again. After we had walked a little further along the path towards the car, I felt that she had gone far enough for one day. It was important that we finished on a positive note.

As we turned and made our way back home Maia returned to the happy hound that she had been before she had her fright. It was encouraging to see that she was able to put it behind her and enjoy the rest of her walk.

We returned to the field the following day. There was only one car parked in the layby. We approached as we had done the day before - walk a few steps, stop and reward, watch the car for a while, then continue. This time we got within 100 metres of the car before I felt we should turn for home. It was vital that Maia stayed calm and relaxed after her fright the day before. As neither Tam nor Maia really wanted to go home, we made our way back across the field and through to the next field. The dogs really seemed to be enjoying themselves, pulling my arms out but enjoying themselves. Tam's big tail was held aloft and Maia's bony little fishhook was pointing sky-wards and they matched strides. After we had walked across the field we turned back to head home. We had almost made it back to the little gate between fields when I saw a lady jogging up behind us. Oh no! I only had enough time to take Maia and Tam about 12 metres off the path before the jogger stopped and shouted out a cheery 'hello' and waved at us. With that Maia went into complete meltdown. When she realised that she couldn't bolt she began spinning round and round at the end of her lead. The lead was twisting tighter and tighter round my hand. I hoped that the jogger would see we were having issues and give us more space. Unfortunately, as we moved away, she followed us. Clearly my message about needing lots of space hadn't got round the whole village yet! I crouched down and got hold of Maia in my arms then surprisingly calmly asked the jogger to continue on their way. Tam did his usual thing and was a great calming influence for Maia but she was really scared and just wanted to go home. I could plan and prepare for most things but we were never going to be able to completely avoid incidents like this.

Maia pulled all the way home but it wasn't through exuberance. The encounter had really shaken her up, but once we returned to the cottage she was quick to settle. While the walk hadn't exactly gone to plan, it gave me loads more information about Maia and her challenges. We were all on a steep learning curve and these blips were inevitable. There was always tomorrow.

I decided to repeat the walk we had the day before but hoped that we wouldn't be chased down by a jogger this time! Maia was very enthusiastic to go out again so I hoped that there was no long term damage done. I put her harness on and she raced down the garden with Tam. All looked good.

We walked through the copse and I was towed up the slope. It was fair to say that Maia's enthusiasm had returned! We walked across the first field to within 20 metres of where the car was parked and apart from being on full-alert, Maia was fine and happy to proceed. We then turned and walked back across the field, through the gate and into the next field. It was with some relief that Maia showed no signs of anxiety entering that field. We continued our walk right across the field and back and didn't see a soul. It was perfect. We needed an incident-free walk and we were lucky enough to get one.

After we got home, I felt that Tam really needed a good run. The problem was that Maia couldn't be left at home on her own yet. After much deliberation I decided I would take Tam out on his own for just a few minutes. He had been so good and tolerant with Maia but it was clear that he needed and deserved a proper run. I had to be very mindful of his emotional disposition as well as Maia's.

I decided to prepare a kong for Maia. Kongs are hollow rubber toys designed to be stuffed with tasty treats. The good thing about them is that if you stuff them properly, they can keep dogs entertained for a while as they try to get the goodies out. I filled Maia's kong with layers of chicken, Tam's kibble and wet dog food and squashed it in so it was quite tightly packed. That should do the job. I set up my phone to video Maia and threw a handful of kibble on the floor for her to find when Tam and I were out. After wrestling with Tam to stop him from eating the kibble I gave Maia the kong, told her to 'stay and be good' and then slipped out of the back door with Tam.

Tam was delighted to be out off-lead. The moment I opened the gate he took off without giving me a second glance. We walked across the field with Tam zig-zagging back and forth and bounding through the long grass. He was having such a great time. We were gone for a bit longer than intended and it pained me to have to call Tam back but he came as soon as I asked. There was just time for one more little treat - something Tam had really missed since Maia's arrival - to have a good soak in the river! As he raced through the copse I saw him run straight down the river bank into the water - then splosh! It is only a small river, approximately three metres wide and perhaps a third of a metre deep but it was enough for Tam to cool his tummy. He waded up and down the river, lapping up the water and then lay down in it. He looked so happy. It might only have been a short walk but it was clear that Tam very much appreciated it.

We made our way back to the cottage and with some trepidation I opened the back door. I was greeted by a slightly wary Maia. The first thing she did was to frantically sniff my hands which seemed a bit odd. It was almost like she wasn't sure if it was me or not. Then Tam appeared and Maia got really excited. She began rapid nose poking in Tam's face while her tail wagged excitedly. What a lovely welcome - for Tam anyway! I made my way to the kitchen and switched off the video recorder. That would make interesting viewing. I scanned the living room and everything seemed in order. The kong was empty and there were just a few pieces of kibble left dotted around the floor which Tam was doing a great job of hoovering up. OK, time to see what Maia had got up to...

The video showed her pacing up and down a couple of times before tucking into her kong. She kept going to check on the back door but she was always quick to return to her kong. I thought that this greedy lurcher's desire for food would be enough of a distraction to prevent her from getting too anxious - and it was. She was worried, but not too worried. This was great as it meant that after our daily family walk I would be able to get Tam out for a short run on his own. As long as she had enough high-value food to keep her occupied I was confident that she should cope OK.

Over the next few weeks I gradually increased the length of Tam's walks so Maia was left for slightly longer periods on her own. It was great that she was learning such an important life skill.

The end of another good day and it was time for bed. Tam led the way upstairs, closely followed by Maia. As I collected my phone and a glass of water I could hear the now familiar pounding of little lurcher paws on the floor above me. It really is amazing how much noise a dainty little lurcher can make. They can be quite boisterous - in a pointy nose kind of way.

As I got to the top of the stairs I was greeted by the now familiar shimmy, play bow and spin, but Maia seemed to engage with a little more vigour than usual. I had a horrible sinking feeling that some-one wasn't ready to settle down and go to sleep yet.

After the dogs had eaten their bedtime treat, Tam took himself off to bed. Just behind him I could see Maia bouncing around with a crazy look on her face. Getting her to settle was going to be fun. I called Maia to her bed and tapped it with my hand, signalling that she should get in. With this she slammed both front feet onto my hand, did a fabulous play bow, grabbed her teddy and darted back into the spare room. Fine! If Maia wanted to play at 11.45pm she could do so on her own. Tam and I needed our beauty sleep.

As I switched off the light I kept hearing Maia bouncing around and pouncing on something. What had she found? It couldn't be any-thing too bad as there wasn't much in there she could reach. I would find out in the morning. After some time, Maia came into my room again, climbed onto her bed, gave it a sniff, turned two circles, flopped down, and didn't move again until morning. Once she's down, she really is out for the count.

The following morning a devastating realisation emerged. It turned out that Maia had been playing with Tam's favourite soft toy 'Lamby'. It was a little soft cuddly toy lamb that he had owned for several years and one that he had carried around with him every-where he went. It was by far his most favourite toy EVER! As I approached Lamby's slightly deflated body I noticed something laying on the carpet beside it - one of Lamby's button eyes. At least she hadn't swallowed it! I checked the other eye and it was clear that Maia had had a go at that one too but it was still hanging on by a thread. Tam came rushing over to assess the damage. Thankfully, Lamby's injuries were not life threatening and he had lived to see another day. I think I needed to have another lesson with Maia about which toys she was allowed to destroy and which she had to leave well alone. Note to self, Maia was not to be trusted around sheep!

It was apparent that Maia was an indoor dog. Yes she loved going out on her walks but apart from that, it seemed to her that there were very few positives to being outside. There was the risk of catching a glimpse of the neighbours going about their business, in their own gardens, or hearing them talking to each other a few metres away. Then there were the flies that insisted on landing on Maia's flank to her great irritation. Then, there was the rain!

Tam is a complete hippo. If the rain is hammering down even if it is near horizontal he doesn't seem to notice. He *loves* it. Those puddles to lie down in were golden retriever heaven. Not so for my skinny wimpy lurcher. Ooooh no! If there was even the slightest chance of rain, just a drop, getting Maia out in the garden became a battle of wills. Now I always considered myself to be pretty strong willed but I am a mere amateur compared to Maia. It had been raining all day and Maia had held her bladder since the night before. She would have to go out to empty eventually and the rain showed no sign of easing off. Somehow I had to get her outside.

I dressed Maia in her nice new waterproof coat, got her all excited and then opened the door. Her whole demeanour changed in an instant. Perhaps I was naïve thinking that would work with such a rain-averse hound. On to Plan B. Chicken! This worked to a point as I was able to lure Maia to just outside the back door and there she stayed. I broke with my own protocol and closed the back door behind her as I knew if I didn't, Maia would be back inside before I could say 'M...'!

I walked up the passageway to the garden, called Maia's name and tried to jolly her along. Nothing. I waved the chicken around but there was no chance she was falling for that one again. Instead she planted herself resolutely by the backdoor and made no attempt to take a step further towards the garden. She looked totally dejected. Head lowered, squinting through the raindrops that fell on her face and twitching her ears whenever a raindrop dared to land on them. It was a pitiful sight. At this point, it is only fair to remind you that I too was standing out in the pouring rain but unlike Maia, I was not wearing a nice new waterproof coat. I was standing there in a lightweight jumper, cotton trousers and crocs! On to Plan C. Wait for as long as it takes. So there we were, at stalemate. Who was going to crack first? For 20 minutes we stood outside in the rain. I was absolutely freezing but having started this, I had to see it through. Eventually Maia cracked. She walked a couple of circles, had a wee and in 10 seconds, our 20 minute stand-off came to an end.

I gave Maia loads of praise for (finally) toileting then opened the door and we both ran inside. First I took off her coat and she was lovely and warm and dry underneath. Then I gave her a sausage treat which are Maia's absolute favourites as technically she had done as I asked. Finally I grabbed a towel and dried off her head and neck. Maia loved it and rubbed her face in the towel doing all the work for me. Then it was time to dry Tam who had been lying out in the grass watching the whole episode unfold. Six towels later and some vigorous rubbing and he was dry-ish. Finally, I peeled off my jumper, took off my waterlogged socks and climbed into some dry clothes. I gave Tam and Maia a quick cuddle then spent the rest of the evening trying to warm up. It had been quite a challenge but at least I had won that battle of wills.

We settled down on the sofa for the evening. After letting me know where she wanted to be stroked, Maia lay flat out while I tickled her tummy. Yes, it's fair to say the balance of power had been restored. I knew my place!

By the end of week three I finally got to witness the moment that I had been waiting and longing for since Maia arrived with us. It was in the evening and I was busy working on my laptop. Maia was lying on the sofa and Tam climbed up onto the sofa at the opposite end from Maia. They both settled and fell asleep. I am not quite sure when it happened as I was engrossed in my work, but when I looked up Maia had turned round and had her head buried in the thick hair on Tam's back. They were both fast asleep and looked so at peace. Aww! I couldn't help myself, it was such a special moment and yes, the tears flowed. This was such a huge breakthrough as Tam was still very unsure how to react to Maia's touch. They stayed snuggled for over an hour. I took a photo of them and have to admit that when I look at the photo now I feel the same emotion that I did when it happened. It really was a wonderful moment.

That evening in her haste to get upstairs before Tam, Maia lost her footing and slipped on the stairs. It didn't really seem to slow her down very much and I thought nothing more of it. It was in the morning when we went out into the garden that I noticed Maia was very slightly lame on her right front leg. It wasn't bad and I was sure she would be fine after a couple of days rest. All I had to do was keep her quiet. The timing was a bit unfortunate as Tam and Maia had started to get on a better and were spending increasing lengths of time out in the garden together. Oh well, it couldn't be helped. It would only be for a few days.

Later that afternoon Tam was doing his usual thing mooching around in the garden and Maia was fast asleep on the sofa so I went to make myself a cup of tea. As I waited for the kettle to boil, I glanced out of the kitchen window just in time to see the dogs flash past - they were enjoying a great game of chase in the garden! Hang on a minute, Maia was meant to be resting. She must have tip-toed right past me. So much for keeping her calm and quiet! I called them in and they were both puffing away looking very pleased with themselves.

Clearly I was going to have to step up my observations on this one. Thankfully no harm was done and after a couple of days Maia was back to normal. Well normal for Maia anyway.

Snuggling on the sofa

SEVENTEEN - Week 4

Our walks, although not very exciting, had been going well. We had started to walk at slightly busier times which gave Maia the opportunity to watch walkers from a comfortable distance. Regular walkers got to recognise us and knew to give us a wide berth and Maia was able to let them get a closer each day without reacting.

As she was becoming more confident I felt that it was time for me to let Tam off the lead so he could have a nice run while Maia stayed with me on the lead. I knew that Tam would come back to us if called, so if Maia got worried help would always be close at hand. After we had negotiated the stile I quietly unclipped Tam's lead. It didn't take him long to realise that he was free and he took off up the slope and across the field. In that moment Maia changed from timid little lurcher into a crazed gazelle! She suddenly leapt forward, launching herself a metre off the ground. Well that was another rather unexpected surprise! We continued walking for a few more strides with Maia pulling my arms out and then she leapt up in the air again. Poor Maia, she was so frustrated that she was restrained while Tam was running free but I couldn't risk letting her off yet. If anything frightened her she would be off in a flash and there was a good chance I'd never see her again. Somehow I had to teach her that staying with me was good and that 'airs above the ground' were not.

I started by rewarding her for keeping all four paws on the ground. When she walked quietly without pulling I gave her loads of praise and a good chunk of chicken. Every time she leapt forwards I gave a quiet 'a-aa' correction then praised and rewarded her for walking nicely again. It took several weeks but gradually Maia understood what I was asking. The number of leaps started to reduce and she would walk nicely for longer before launching herself again. It was definitely improving, as was the pain in my back and shoulders. Thankfully before long Maia had stopped leaping. Learning to walk on the lead without pulling would take a little longer.

I felt it was time that Maia had another visitor so I invited Barb round to see her again. It had been three weeks since Barb's last visit so it was going to be interesting to see how Maia would react to her now. We followed the same protocol as for all house guests. Come in, get past the welcoming committee, sit on the left hand seat on the sofa and completely ignore Maia. On Barb's previous visit Maia had considered joining her on the sofa but wasn't quite brave enough. There was no such hesitation this time. Very quickly, Maia climbed up on the sofa and lay down beside Barb. Barb had a few minutes to get comfortable before Maia started nudging her for attention. What a difference three weeks makes!

The dogs were coping really well when left alone now. My concerns about Tam's anxiety when I left the cottage had eased and he now looked a little more relaxed. He usually settled and dozed off about 10 minutes after I left. By week four I had built up the time they were being left alone for up to 2½ hours, twice daily. I was still recording them when I went out but there wasn't much to see. After the first few minutes of activity they both fell asleep - it's a dog's life.

While the dogs were learning to be left alone I had been occupying myself by going on shopping or sight-seeing trips but I was starting to run out of ideas of where to go to waste time. I ended up visiting all the small local museums and places of interest that I had always intended to visit but never had. It was almost like being on holiday.

On one occasion I went shopping and returned with three carrier bags of groceries. Maia's bag rustling training had been going really well but she wasn't completely over her fear. She didn't particularly like carrier bags and avoided walking too close to them. I could carry the shopping past her and she would follow me in to the kitchen at a safe distance. She was starting to learn that bags could be a good. That was until today.

As I went into the kitchen I plonked the bags on the worktops and went to hang up my coat by the back door. Unfortunately I didn't check to make sure that the bags were secure when I put them down. Just as I left the kitchen two of the bags fell off the work top and crashed to the floor. I rushed back to the kitchen to see Maia racing round the living room, tail clamped between her legs, trembling all over in total panic. I could have kicked myself for making such a silly mistake. I went to reassure Maia but it was going to take more than that for her to forgive me. She wouldn't let me anywhere near her. Now I admit that it was technically my fault, but it was an accident. I wasn't even in the room when it happened! I tried again to calm Maia down but I wasn't making much progress so Tam had to stand in for me. He went over to Maia and stood quietly next to her and after a minute or two she was back on the sofa.

It was hours before Maia eventually forgave me, but it left her wary of going back into the kitchen. Despite my reassurances, she had no intention of going in there unless she really had to. It took days for Maia to overcome her fear of the kitchen and return to how she was before the bag incident. As with many of Maia's issues, time and chicken were great healers.

On a more positive note, there had been no toileting accidents in the cottage for nine days. Better still, Maia was actually starting to indicate when she needed to go out in the garden. It was like the penny had finally dropped. Whenever she did, she was welcomed back into the cottage like a champion, like she was the best dog in the world (which of course she is, along with Tam!) I went so over the top with praise that she started to get really over-excited when she came in, rushing round the living room, tail wagging frantically, play bowing and spinning. It made me feel so happy for this weird hound.

Maia's itching continued to be an issue and I wasn't convinced it was entirely behavioural. I contacted my vet and we agreed to treat her as if it was an allergic reaction to something and tried giving her some medication to settle it down. Thankfully it seemed to do the trick. Within a couple of hours Maia's skin returned to normal light pink colour and she greatly reduced her nibbling. Just what I needed - two dogs with allergies!

Maia in her walking kit

EIGHTEEN - Week 5

Maia was really enjoying her walks but she was getting increasingly frustrated. Tam was running ahead and she wanted to join him but I still couldn't risk letting her off-lead as she was still unpredictable on walks. She could be walking nicely with her head and tail up, pulling like a tank then suddenly she would take fright at something, start backing up and then panic. Sometimes I could see what she was scared of - a walker for example - but other times I couldn't work out what it was. I knew that if she was off the lead at that point she would bolt. There aren't many fences on the open farmland that surrounds our cottage so if Maia did get away from me, she would be loose in thousands of acres of open country. It just wasn't worth the risk.

The problem remained. Maia really needed a good run so I decided to book a slot in a secure dog walking field. The field wasn't huge but it was certainly big enough for Maia to have a good run, so long as I was brave enough to unclip her lead when we got there. It had secure dog-proof fencing round the perimeter and Maia, Tam and I would be the only ones there. Perfect for Maia's first outing.

The field was about a half an hour drive away which was a little further than I'd hoped but it was certainly doable. There were just a few issues. We always went out for walks via the back garden so Maia hadn't been out to the front of the cottage since the day she arrived. There are some very steep steps from my front door up to my driveway and at the top is a busy road. How would Maia cope with all the traffic passing by? I also didn't know how she would react to my car. If she panicked on the drive, there was very little space for manoeuvre. Another issue was how Tam and Maia would cope when sitting next to each other on the back seat of my rather small car. It was going to be quite snug. Tam doesn't travel that well at the best of times. Would the extra stress of sharing the back seat with his little sister make his travel sickness worse? I only had four days to work on it and the clock was ticking.

I chose the quietest time of the day to introduce Maia to the big wide world beyond the front door for the first time. After checking and double checking that her harness and collar were secure and grabbing an enormous handful of chicken, I tacked up Tam and opened the door. Tam was getting bored with his restricted walks and was only too happy to go somewhere different so he led the way. After slight hesitation, Maia ventured out after him.

I waited for a few minutes at the foot of the steps to give Maia a chance to take everything in. She looked quite anxious but didn't shut down. She started sniffing the air and seemed curious to learn more about her surroundings. I left the front door open so she had an escape route if it all got too much for her. Tam was perplexed as to why we were just standing outside and not actually *going* anywhere. Despite his confusion, his self-control was impressive and he stood quietly next to Maia which gave her loads of confidence. It was time to make our way up the steps.

Tam led the way. Maia hopped up the bottom two steps but then hesitated. She was understandably very wary and needed time to take it all in. I was happy to wait and reassured her until she was ready to continue. It wasn't long before she climbed up the next few steps and after another brief hesitation, she cautiously continued to the top. Rather surprisingly, she didn't seem at all concerned about the traffic whizzing by.

We walked round to the rear door on the driver's side and I opened it. Tam was quick to jump in and sat on his usual side on the back seat. Seeing Tam in the car encouraged Maia to approach it and have a good sniff. Whenever she was unsure her nose always went into overdrive. I really didn't want to lift Maia into the car as it had to be her decision, and when she was ready she hopped in.

It had taken less than ten minutes, lots of praise and some chicken, to get both dogs in the car which was pretty good going for our first attempt. After they had been sitting in the car for a few minutes, it was time for us to go back to the cottage. In order to give Maia as much confidence as possible I asked Tam to get out the car first and Maia was happy to follow. We made our way back down the steps and into the cottage. It had all gone way better than I could have wished for.

Over the next couple of days we had a few more rehearsals before our trip to the field. Tam and Maia stayed in the car for slightly longer periods each time to get used to sharing the back seat. It was a bit tight but they were working out where they could sit to be comfortable. It turned out that Tam was a bit better at sharing than Maia. After a few minutes sitting in the car I looked over my shoulder to see Maia reclining right across the whole back seat with poor Tam sitting squashed against the door. I called Maia back over to her side. He must have been really uncomfortable but he didn't complain and made no attempt to get Maia to move over himself, he just waited for me to notice and rescue him. The next stage was to start the engine to make sure that Maia was happy with the noise and vibration. As I turned the key in the ignition she didn't bat an eyelid. After our little training sessions I felt confident that Tam and Maia would cope with the journey to the field.

At last the day arrived for our first family outing. It was gloriously warm and sunny so I had booked to go to the field in the evening when it would be slightly cooler. I was concerned about how the dogs would cope with the heat. Maia had such a thin coat it offered very little protection from the sun. As for Tam, even in his summer coat he looked like a polar bear so I had to be careful to make sure that he didn't overheat.

Finally it was time to go. I added extra time to allow for any issues with Maia getting in the car or any traffic that might slow us down. I was confident that I knew where the field was and had read and re-read all the instructions about how to gain entry so I was pretty sure that everything would go according to plan.

Maia chose to sit very close to Tam in the car and at times leant against him. Unfortunately Tam values his personal space so he wasn't comfortable with the intrusion but he tolerated it well. I didn't want to push Tam's good nature, so if Maia tried to hog the back seat again I was ready to step in. The last thing I wanted was for Tam to feel he had to correct Maia himself as that could really compromise their relationship. I kept a close eye on them during the journey through my rear-view mirror and they both seemed reasonably settled. If these trips were going to be a regular event, I was going to have to consider getting a more spacious car!

We arrived right on time. I wasn't sure who was more excited - me or the dogs. Right, deep breath - this was it! I opened the door and unclipped the dogs' seatbelts. Then just as we had practised I asked Tam to jump out first. He didn't need asking twice. He launched himself out of the car like something possessed! He caught me quite off guard and I only just managed to keep hold of him. Cheeky boy! Then I asked Maia to jump out of the car which she did with enthusiasm.

My plan was to walk them round the field once on the lead so they could see where the boundary fence was and get their bearings. Then I would let Tam off first and depending on how Maia was reacting, hopefully I could let her off too. Well that was the plan. A month of confinement had taken its toll on Tam. He was so excited to be out that he went into overdrive, trying to run this way then that way. He seemed to forget he was still on the lead.

Having fun ...

... and cramping Tam's style, at the
secure dog field

We got to the gate and entered the field. There were so many new smells Tam didn't know where to begin. Maia was taking a more considered approach and was taking time to sniff the air and take a good look at her surroundings. We started to make our way round the field but it was clear that the two dogs had very different needs. Tam could barely control himself - he just needed to go and explore. All his obedience training went out the window and he couldn't focus on anything at all so I decided to admit defeat and let him go off-lead. It was the best decision for all of us.

As Tam disappeared across the field I continued walking with Maia on the lead. To my delight she seemed really happy and excited. Her tail was up and she was pulling enthusiastically. She was clearly just as keen as Tam to go and explore but I wanted to give her just a few more minutes to get her bearings. Tam had gone into marking over-drive and was stopping to mark every few metres. I really don't know where it all comes from! It was wonderful to see him enjoying himself. It was another reminder about the stress and pressure he had been under since having a new little sister.

Maia and I completed a full circuit of the field and I felt that the big moment had finally arrived. She had behaved impeccably to that point, I had to make that huge leap of faith and let her run free. As my finger hovered over the trigger clip on the lead I felt such mixed emotions. It was the moment I had been waiting for but there was also every chance that I might not be able to catch her again. I had the field to myself for another 20 minutes so surely I would be able to catch her? I had to be brave, trust Maia and just do it.

I unclipped the lead and in a flash she was gone. It was amazing. This slightly clumsy fearful hound ran round the perimeter of the whole field at top speed with such beauty and grace it really was the most wonderful sight to behold - and goodness, she was fast! After a couple of laps she came running straight towards me. She skimmed past me missing me by a few centimetres and then came to a halt right behind me. She was puffing really hard after her exertions but the look on her face was priceless. She was literally grinning from ear to ear. I have to admit that I had tears in my eyes. It was really quite overwhelming. Not only had it been wonderful to see Maia having a good run but it was also the most amazing feeling seeing her run back to me to tell me all about it. It was confirmation that our relationship was on the right track.

I started to walk round the field with Maia jogging along next to me giving my hands the odd poke as if to share with me just how happy she was. She was absolutely beaming. I wasn't the only one who had been waiting for so long for that moment. Maia must have also dreamt of this day and took full advantage of the opportunity. As soon as she managed to catch her breath she was off again, lapping the field at top speed before hurtling back to me. One thing quickly became clear – recall wasn't going to be an issue. I waited for her to get to the furthest possible point in the field before calling her and she flew back to me. I took my phone and began videoing this momentous occasion. Trying to keep Maia in frame when she was belting round the field at top speed with sudden random changes of direction was no mean feat! She was so fast I could barely keep up with her and I was starting to feel dizzy as I panned across the field trying to keep her in shot. Every crazy high speed zoomies circuit ended with Maia running back to me which was a relief.

Once she had got her breath back - for the fourth time - she decided to go and join Tam. After sprinting over to him she slowed to a jog and then slotted in neatly behind him. I'm not sure Tam was too thrilled about having Maia tag along but he carried on regardless.

Cosy in the back-seat

They trotted around the field together and when Tam stopped to check out a smell, Maia stopped. She was definitely cramping his style. When Tam went to sniff something, Maia thrust her pointy nose in front of his to see what had caught his attention. I am sure Tam was finding Maia's behaviour a bit irritating but he tolerated it.

As they were trotting round the field, Tam spotted something and ran at top speed to go and investigate. Maia took off in hot pursuit yet within three of her huge strides had already overtaken him. Her excitement was just too great to contain so she took off across the field in zoomies mode and did another couple of circuits. Tam tried to join her but he was way too slow. The realisation hit him very quickly but he is smarter than he looks. As Maia sprinted in huge sweeping circles round the field, Tam kept to a much smaller circle in the middle and tried to cut her off as she flew past. He put up a good challenge but it wasn't long before he gave up and went back to his marking. With that, Maia flopped down in the grass, rolled onto her side and took time out to catch her breath.

It was with a little sadness that I watched Tam and Maia in the field. It brought it home how different they were and how hard it was going to be for them to play together. Tam would never be able to keep up with Maia and Maia didn't see any point in trotting when she could be sprinting. I really hoped they would find some middle ground but it would mean they would both have to adapt their own unique styles, or they faced a lifetime of walking together alone.

A time check showed we had just five more minutes in the field - enough time for one more lap. As we returned to the gate, I clipped the leads onto their harnesses and returned to the car. Tam jumped in first followed by Maia. They both looked so satisfied and content. Our first trip to the field had been a huge success.

I'm not sure how they managed it but on the drive home, they both lay down on the back seat of the car, nose to tail with Maia resting her head on Tam's back. I barely heard a sound out of them for the entire journey. Once home, Tam lay in his favourite cool spot in the kitchen and dozed off. Maia took up position on a throw on the floor right in front of me. Then - I will never forget it - she rested her long pointy nose on the throw and looked up at me with that same soft look she had given me when she was in kennels. It was that look of real knowing, complete trust and unconditional love. She held her gaze for about 15 minutes until she eventually fell asleep. I watched her as she slept and my heart was close to bursting. It was such a privilege to share my home with such an incredible soul.

Despite having a great time at the field, I felt trouble brewing. Tam had been such an amazing support to Maia. He had been gentle and forgiving and he had made many sacrifices but I felt some unease bubbling. The honeymoon period was over and realisation that Maia would be staying had started to set in. The changes were subtle but they were enough for alarm bells to start to ring.

I noticed that Tam had started to lay in doorways, or position himself in such a way that Maia couldn't get past him. He would also block the passageway from the garden to the cottage leaving Maia trapped outside. Tam knew that he could control her very easily just with his presence and that Maia would never challenge him. Tam never showed any overt aggression but this door blocking was a very deliberate, passive-aggressive move on his part. Whenever he lay down it was always in a place where I would have to correct him. He wasn't being naughty or nasty but it showed that he was insecure and unhappy. I needed to take this really seriously.

Whenever I saw Tam blocking access I would ask him to get up and move somewhere more appropriate. He could still be close to me without blocking Maia's way. I didn't tell him off because to Tam, it made perfect sense, but it wasn't acceptable behaviour. At the same time I looked to find ways to strengthen their relationship. I tried to encourage things that they could enjoy doing together but their communication issues and vastly different play styles were still making play difficult.

The mutual bone-chewing was going well. Most evenings they would settle down for a session. They usually lay very close to each other and often had paws or tails touching while they chewed. After a while they would swap bones by mutual agreement. It was clear that they wanted to spend time together but they didn't really know how to go about it. The trips to the secure dog field were having a positive effect on their relationship as they could run, share sniffs and relax free from the confines of my cottage. For a few days after each visit there was definitely slightly less tension between the two but sadly it was going to take more to resolve all their issues.

Despite their difficulties there were some lovely moments between the two of them when they let their guard down. I saw a particularly touching moment when I played back the recording after a shopping trip. It only lasted a moment but I saw Tam walk across the living room and go over to Maia to sniff noses with her. Luckily, she reciprocated and it was such a lovely gesture. It was significant that Tam went out of his way to go and say Hello to Maia especially as I wasn't there to support him and it was a tiny glimmer of hope that these two might be able to work things out ... eventually.

The following evening we had a huge breakthrough. Tam was very guarded about his personal space yet that evening the dogs lay down next to each other and Maia rested her chin on Tams paw. Tam looked very surprised and didn't quite know how to react. He started to look a bit worried so I reassured him, he held his position and started to relax. They stayed in that position for some time and then fell asleep muzzle to muzzle. This was the breakthrough I had been waiting for and I have to admit to crying happy tears.

Our walks in the fields had been going so well, I felt that it was time to broaden Maia's horizons and explore the beautiful countryside that surrounds us. Next to the layby there is a narrow kissing gate. It was a challenge to navigate as only one dog could go through at a time. Tam went through first to show Maia how it was done and then it was Maia's turn. Logical thinking and problem solving were not Maia's forte and she struggled to work out how to go through. She would take a couple of steps forward, lose her nerve and back up and then go forward again. It was quite a dance. Eventually, with lots of encouragement, she worked it out and we were all through.

Tam led the way and we set off at quite a clip. The lane is usually nice and quiet and after a few hundred metres we joined a pretty bridle path. Both dogs seemed to be really enjoying their walk until we walked past a house with a sweeping gravel drive behind a tall hedge. Just as we were walking past, a car started and crunched along the drive. Maia panicked, went into reverse and tried to run. It could have been the sound of the car on the gravel or the fact that she could hear the noise but couldn't see where it was coming from that scared her. I took her in my arms and I could feel her heart pounding. I held her and sent her some healing until she settled. It seemed to work. We all stood quietly for a while. Her automatic reaction was to run but, her natural curiosity started to take over and she began to show interest in her surroundings again. Tam clearly thought it was all rather boring but by this time he had resigned himself to having boring walks when out with Maia.

Once Maia had regained her composure we continued our walk up the track and then turned home. At the kissing gate, Maia followed Tam through surprisingly easily considering the problems she had the first time, but I think that was more luck than judgment!

As we walked back across the field Maia's confidence returned. I let Tam off so he could have a bit of a run and it gave me a chance to do a little lead training with Maia. She responded really well and there were brief moments of loose lead walking, which was a huge improvement on her usual pull and leap walking style.

Later that evening Tam and Maia had a lovely moment that was initiated by Tam. They had just enjoyed a synchronised bone-chewing session and had settled down to have a doze. Tam gently rested his chin on Maia's hind leg. It was a deliberate move on Tam's part and it can't have been easy for him as he still found physical contact with Maia so awkward. Unfortunately, Maia has skinny little legs and when Tam rested his huge heavy retriever head on her leg she didn't find it very comfortable so moved her leg out of the way. But Tam wasn't ready to give up so he tried again. This time he chose to rest his head on Maia's tail instead! That was clearly more acceptable to Maia and within seconds they had both fallen asleep.

Tam had pushed through his uncertainty about touching Maia and realised that she might have her uses after all. She might be a weird bony hound but she did make quite a convenient headrest.

Friends at last!

NINETEEN - Week 6

It had only taken six weeks but I was starting to see real breakthroughs in Maia's training. She had finally started to understand the concept of doing something to *earn* a reward. This could help our training no end. Toilet training was now complete. Not only was Maia taking herself out to the garden when she needed to go but she was actually doing it on cue. She was getting much less fearful of her trigger objects such as carrier bags and cardboard boxes and her confidence with humans was steadily growing. She was also getting more relaxed around me and our relationship was going from strength to strength. There was however one big issue that I would have to address, sooner rather than later.

Maia's nails were beginning to look a bit long so I had to prepare to have her nails clipped. The last thing I wanted was for her nails to grow too long and then split or tear. Most dogs need to have their nails clipped every month or two throughout their lifetime yet it is surprising how many dogs, and their owners, struggle with this. A combination of tickly paws, pain and perhaps the fear of a nick of the sensitive quick in the nail can all combine to make dogs really fearful and in some cases quite aggressive when this is being done. I wanted to make sure that Maia was happy and consenting from the start. It would have been much quicker to physically restrain her and then quickly clip her nails but I was determined that she would never feel that powerless again. She had come so far it would be a real betrayal of trust.

The problem was that her fear was so deeply ingrained, I couldn't start her training until I felt she was robust enough to cope with it. It could take weeks or even months for Maia to accept having her nails clipped. I had to start from scratch so I broke the procedure down into lots of tiny easily achievable steps. As we worked through each of the steps I watched Maia very closely ensuring she was happy and confident before moving on to the next step.

To prepare Maia, I started off by gently touching and stroking her legs and paws. She seemed absolutely fine with that so I moved onto touching her long finger-like toes. Still no reaction - so far so good! Then as I went to hold her toe Maia let out a tremendous yelp and snatched her paw away from me. Her reaction was completely unexpected. She had made it very clear that she didn't want me to hold her toes so I went back a couple of steps. I started by touching her legs and paws when we were sitting on the sofa watching TV. It was all very relaxed, low key and spontaneous. I wanted Maia to learn that when I touched her paws it was no different from when I stroked her neck or tummy, it was just a little bit more ticklish!

Once Maia was happy for me to stroke her paws I started to gently manipulate her toes again. There was no reaction so I moved on to touch her nails. All was going really well until I gently took hold of her nail. She immediately pulled her paw away and rolled back in a very submissive gesture. She was clearly worried. It could be that she anticipated what might come next or there was a chance that she had some pain in her digits. Either way, she had communicated to me that she wasn't comfortable so I had to show her that I was listening. I reverted back to stroking her body and legs where she was comfortable and would try again later.

After about a week and many mini toe-touching sessions, I felt that Maia was ready for me to manipulate her toes again. I started very gently, watching very closely for any signs of anxiety, waiting for the yelp but thankfully it didn't come. Maia was already much less defensive. We were definitely making progress.

I continued to handle her toes for a few more days and she was getting more relaxed about it. I felt that she might be ready to move on to the next step so I manipulated her toe into the position to clip her nail. I didn't have my nail clippers with me. I just wanted to get her used to having her toes moved into the required position. With that Maia gave me a clear 'no'. She yelped and pulled her paw away. Tam had been lying fast asleep on the floor, but as soon as he heard Maia yelp he was at her side in a flash. He knew that Maia needed him. So, stroking toes OK, holding toe up as if to clip nail - definitely not OK.

While I was working on handling Maia's toes I started to introduce her to the nail clippers. When she saw them she looked worried so I thought she might prefer a nail dremel instead. Dremels are like mini sanders that grind the nail down instead of clipping it off. Even though it was very light there was still a slight vibration that Maia would have to get used to. There was a bigger hurdle. My dremel made a very quiet buzzing sound, similar to the buzzing of a bee. Unfortunately Tam is really scared of bees since getting stung when he was a puppy, so as soon as he heard the buzzing dremel he was out of the room like a shot. That wasn't quite the calm, confident, reassuring influence I was looking for! So I had a choice - continue getting Maia used to the clippers or teach Maia AND Tam to get used to the dremel. On balance I decided on the nail clippers!

To help Maia get over her fear of the clippers I put them on the sofa next to me so she could have a good look at them. It's easy to forget to let our dogs examine the equipment we use on them, so they always remain suspicious of it. She gave them a good sniff and poked them with her nose. It was surprising how much time she spent inspecting them.

I kept the clippers on the arm of the sofa for a few days and Maia learnt that they weren't anything to be frightened of. Over the next few days I began to gently stroke Maia with the clippers starting with her body, then moving on to her legs and finally her toes. After this training, Maia was no longer afraid of the clippers and was happy for me to handle them around her without reacting. We were getting closer to our goal but I still had to teach her to accept the actual act of clipping her nails.

Whenever Tam spotted the nail clippers, he came over and sat by the sofa and rested his huge head right next to Maia. They were definitely in this together. Tam didn't mind having his nails clipped so he was a great role model. I clipped his nails in front of Maia so she could watch and see that Tam wasn't the least bit worried and got a food reward after. Perhaps nail clips weren't so bad after all?

As the weeks progressed I was getting a little concerned as Maia's nails seemed to be growing longer by the day. She would accept me touching and manipulating her toes, separating her toes, holding the nail and touching her toes and nails with the clippers but I was starting to feel the pressure. Just when I was starting to get really worried, I saw a shift in Maia's behaviour and felt she was ready for an actual nail clip. I ran my hand gently down Maia's leg, fiddled around with her toes, took her nail and then 'clip'! Maia gave out a massive yelp but by that time it was done. I leapt of the sofa, with Maia in hot pursuit, excitedly praised her like she had just done the best thing EVER. We ran to the treat cupboard and I gave Maia her favourite treat. Tam took full advantage of Maia's success and got a treat too. After Maia had gobbled up her reward we went into the garden and had a game. Phew. One nail down, seventeen to go!

Maia's yelp was an automatic reaction but it was loud and really made me jump. I don't think it was pain related. It was more likely to be the anticipation of pain. It would take time for her to realise that the pain she was anticipating would never come. The big test would be to see her reaction when I tried to clip another nail the next day. The next afternoon, I followed my usual approach so that everything was predictable for Maia. I took it nice and slowly to check that she was coping well with everything and then 'clllllip.' Goodness her nails were hard. Two down! As before, the moment I had clipped the nail we all ran to the kitchen to get Maia's reward. It took a little time but gradually she started to understand that if she could be brave and tolerate the clip, she would be well rewarded.

I clipped one nail a day for several days before building up to two or three, and after each nail I gave Maia an over the top amount of praise, her favourite treat and a game. It took just over two months of repetitive work but we got there in the end. Maia is now co-operative and consenting when she has a nail clip. I show her which leg I need and she holds her paw up for me and then patiently waits for the 'clip'. It was proof again that patient reward based training can lead to long-term positive behaviour change.

Maia had been coping really well with all my female visitors, so it was time to up the ante and start introducing her to more men. She was getting on very well with my neighbour John now after spending many hours spying on him through the gate. She was happy to stand right next to me as we chatted over the fence but she was still wary if he tried to talk to her.

I decided to invite my friend Dan over to come and meet Maia. As with all my previous visitors Dan had been briefed of all the dos and don'ts during his visit. He had to sit in the visitor's seat on the sofa and *completely* ignore Maia. Now Dan was one of Tam's very favourite people. He always played with Tam and he played rough - really rough - just as Tam liked it. It can be easy to get a bit cocky when playing with Tam as his reactions aren't terribly fast. It's actually quite easy to grab his muzzle or the scruff of his neck in play, but if you get the timing wrong and find yourself on the receiving end of a mistimed air snaps, it can make your eyes water. Or if you take your attention away for just a second you can quickly find yourself on the receiving end of one of Tam's right hook face swipes. I have a scar for my error of judgment when I under-estimated my opponent during a rough and tumble game. Don't be fooled by that fluffy, teddy bear exterior. Just beneath the surface there is a crocodile with attitude just waiting to burst out!

After a morning of preparations it was time for Dan's visit. This was going to be a big test for Maia. Not only was she going to have to cope with the arrival of a male stranger, she would also be contend-ing with a very noisy and ridiculously over-excited welcome from turbo Tam.

As Dan entered the cottage Maia's reaction surprised me. Instead of running to the den, she came and stood right behind me. This was a huge change as she came to me for reassurance and protection instead of running away. My message of 'if in doubt, come to me' seemed to be sinking in. Mind you, these were exceptional circumstances as Tam had totally lost it and gone completely wild!

It didn't take long before the need for comfort and smell of chicken persuaded Maia to return to her rightful place on the sofa. Dan did a great job of ignoring her, not that he had much choice as Tam was commanding his full attention. Eventually Tam, exhausted from wrestling with Dan, settled down and gave me the opportunity to carefully introduce Dan to Maia. To help raise her opinion of Dan I gave him some chicken and he started to offer little pieces to Maia. After brief hesitation she started to take it.

Considering how fearful she was of men she coped amazingly well. The only time she looked really worried during the whole of his visit was when he looked at her as he gave her some chicken. Her facial expression changed in an instant and she refused to accept the chicken despite already having taken plenty of pieces from him moments before. Dan offered her another piece of chicken being careful not to look at her and she took it willingly. It was great that despite having a little wobble she quickly bounced back from it.

A few hours into Dan's visit and Maia seemed quite settled next to him so I suggested he give her a stroke on her shoulder. She jumped when he first touched her but after that she started to relax and accept his touch. As the afternoon progressed, I could see Maia's demeanour changing as her confidence grew. After just a few hours she was bold enough to give Dan a poke when he wasn't quick enough when dispensing chicken. As Dan's visit came to an end, I reflected on the day. Maia had made fantastic progress, Tam was sublimely happy and Dan had escaped with no serious injuries, just one minor flesh wound. Perfect!

After all the pressures of the day and several hours on the sofa Maia was in a playful mood. She had started to come out of herself and we were seeing more of her playful side emerging. I was sitting on the floor in the living room having a really rough game with Tam when to my great surprise Maia looked like she wanted to join in. After watching us for a few minutes, she was getting increasingly excited. She was bouncing around and generally getting swept up in Tam's manic energy. She wanted to play with us but she wasn't quite sure how to go about it. In an attempt to get involved Maia did a lovely play bow making it clear that she wanted to join in but she still didn't quite dare to take the plunge. Admittedly, Tam was flashing his teeth and throwing himself around so it would take a very courageous effort for Maia to elbow her way into this game.

Then all of a sudden I felt a really hard double blow to my back. I looked round just in time to see Maia balance on her haunches and then deliver another double thwack to my back with her front legs. It was a move that could only be described as a karate-chop and boy did it hurt! Her eyes were laughing and this was clearly Maia's idea of play. I had to stop my game with Tam so I had both hands free to deflect the blows. Perhaps I should have pointed out to Maia that this kind of 'play' wasn't appropriate, but it was so funny to see the silly giddy look on her face that I couldn't help but laugh. We could moderate her play style at a later date.

Maia's playful mood continued and finally, for the first time Tam and Maia had a proper game playing with the *same* toy at the *same* time. Well when I say toy, I actually mean my reusable shopping bag which Tam had stolen from my handbag. They had a great tug of war with it. Tam was being his usual careful and gentle self. Maia on the other hand was giving it all she had! I watched as she strained with all her might to take it from Tam while Tam was barely making any effort at all. In the end, Tam let Maia win and I had to step in quickly to reclaim the bag before Maia could rip it to pieces. It was the first reasonably rough game Maia had played with Tam that hadn't ended in a dramatic houndy yelp and a quick retreat. You had better watch out Tam. Little Maia has changed!

TWENTY - Week 7

Tam and Maia were getting a bit bored with their walks around the fields and up the bridleway so I decided to take them somewhere new. There is an old disused railway line that runs parallel to the road in front of my cottage that is a really lovely walk. It is very pretty and mostly shaded by trees so it's particularly nice on hot sunny days. There were only two potential issues. The first was that we had to cross a pretty busy road to get onto the footpath. The second was that it was popular with walkers, joggers and cyclists so chances of us meeting someone were quite high and there wasn't much room for us to get out of the way. Maia definitely had days where she felt adventurous and confident and days when she seemed a lot more insecure. As always, where we went and for how long would be dictated by her. Today seemed an adventurous day so it seemed the right day to go somewhere new.

We set out through the field but instead of turning right up the lane, we turned left towards the main road. Tam was delighted to be going up to the railway track again. It had been a while since we had been able to walk there and he had a lot of catching up to do. I kept stopping to give Maia the choice about whether she was happy to continue and each time she indicated that she was. As we approached the road I hung back to check for traffic. Once there was a suitable gap, I took the dogs over the road. As we crossed, Maia saw something in the road and tried to stop and take a better look at it. That really wasn't such a sensible idea on a road with such fast moving traffic. I called her and she immediately jogged to catch up, poked my hand with her nose and looked up at me with a big grin on her face.

We joined the path that wound its way up a gentle slope past a small yard of horses. I know the horses very well and as usual they came over for a head rub. Maia didn't seem to react to them. Clearly horses were OK. We carried on up the path and joined the main track where I let Tam run off-lead. It was so beautiful with the sun shining through the trees. Maia coped brilliantly. True to form she tried to pull me along the track in an attempt to keep up with Tam but she listened to my corrections and started to walk nicely.

As we walked up the track we came across three male cyclists. One was mending a puncture and the other two were sitting on the ground chatting. This would be quite a test for Maia. Tam was quick to run over to them and offer his assistance. As usual he got a warm reception. He has this knack of making people love him and even if they aren't particularly fond of dogs. I guess you've either got it or you haven't! Maia was watching intently but she didn't back off. I am sure that she was learning through watching Tam. When she saw him run up to strangers and enjoy the interactions it gave her confidence.

As we approached, I positioned myself between Maia and the men to act as a barrier and help her feel safer. She was quite tense as she passed them but made no attempt to flee. Tam provided a great distraction so we passed almost unnoticed. Perfect. After I had managed to prise Tam away from his new friends, we continued a little way up the path before turning back and heading for home. Sadly the cyclists had moved on, but it had been a great experience for Maia to have seen them.

As we made our way back towards the main road, Maia spotted a large pigeon feather. She couldn't have been more delighted. She picked it up, tossed it in the air and pounced on it before carrying it all the way back to the road. It was lovely to see her relaxed enough to play. We crossed the road again and Maia made a dive to the same spot she had when we crossed before. At that moment I saw a car coming towards us quite quickly. It's funny how these things seem to play out in slow motion. Dear little Maia was blissfully unaware of the fate that could befall us all if she didn't tear herself away from the spot and get out of the road! Luckily, after one last sniff Maia trotted across the road and we escaped without incident. It was great that Maia was confident enough to investigate an interesting smell on an unfamiliar walk - even though she could have got us all killed in the process!

It struck me how far Maia had come. She had reached another little milestone in her ongoing rehab and it was a clear indicator that she was ready to go out and explore more of the big wide world.

Tam and Maia were now spending most evenings lying next to each other while they chewed bones or played with their toys. It was fascinating to watch them as they worked things out. If they got a bit stuck and weren't sure what to do, one of them would take the initiative and pick up a bone or toy, which would prompt the other to do the same. They found a way that they could continue to spend time together without any awkwardness. They were still usually too cautious to play with the *same* soft toy at the same time, but different toys was for now a pretty good compromise.

There had been really positive signs that both dogs really wanted to play together. If Maia was feeling playful she would roll on her back on the sofa and start squirming on her back with a silly grin on her face and long skinny legs flailing. That would draw Tam to her like a bee to honey, but as Tam got to the sofa he was met by a series of crazed karate chops. As Maia rained down blows on his head and face she often ended up with a paw pressed against his throat or a knee over his eyes. Maia loves these 'games' but I was (and actually still am) really quite concerned that one day Tam could lose an eye. I used to tell Tam to be gentle when playing with Maia but it turns out that she is perfectly capable of looking after herself! I think it is Tam who needs protection - some sort of safety specs perhaps?

Tam wasn't at all put off by being repeatedly pummelled by Maia's whacks. The only problem was that he couldn't really retaliate so it was a bit one-sided. All he could do was rub his face against Maia's face and engage in a bit of polite and careful air snapping. Tam's attempts at play were a little less successful. He would wait for her to join him on the floor then he would roll on his back with his legs in the air. His floppy jowls succumbed to gravity, exposing his rather splendid set of teeth, and he got a really manic look in his eyes. He then tried to roll closer to Maia to encourage her to play but that was enough to send her retreating back to the sofa. To be honest I can't really blame her. Tam weighs nearly twice as much as she does and I have been on the receiving end of what happens when Tam gets 'playful.'

These games were so wonderful to watch. On some occasions Tam would be lying on the floor and Maia would come over and whack him. On others, they would lie down on the floor together and do a few air snaps and paw swipes. On one occasion, Tam nibbled very gently on Maia's ear. Maia responded by biting down really hard on his ear and then gave it a really good death shake. That hound is savage! Sadly most of these games did still end the same way - Maia getting a bit overwhelmed, letting out a blood curdling yelp, and running back to the sofa. GAME OVER.

On some occasions this reaction might have been justified. Perhaps Tam had got a little clumsy and rolled over onto Maia's legs or tail, but it still didn't warrant quite such a dramatic reaction. There were many occasions when I saw that Tam hadn't actually made any physical contact with Maia at all before she got overwhelmed, yelped and ended the game. It was great that they were both trying but they just couldn't work out how to play together.

Tam and Maia had also been spending more time lying next to each other and, oh so slowly, Tam was getting a bit less defensive when Maia tried to snuggle. She was very tentative but on one occasion rested her head on Tam's leg and fell asleep. Tam looked up at me as if to say 'heeeelp!' but I reassured him and he fell asleep too. Then there was another occasion where they were lying on the floor and Maia rolled over a little closer to Tam and he shuffled closer to Maia and they ended up falling asleep lying cheek to cheek. Cue blurry eyes again. Overall their relationship was still positive and still going in the right direction, and I was cautiously optimistic that they could eventually be really good friends.

Sighthounds are renowned for their grace and poise. Watching them run it is like poetry in motion - they are perfectly stream-lined and superbly balanced. A picture of pure beauty. When they are resting however, they look a little less spectacular. Maia has a tendency to sleep with her mouth slightly open - sometimes with her tongue hanging out - revealing her little incisors in a rather disconcerting toothy grin. To add to the picture she also often squashes her nose into the arm of the sofa so the end of her nose is pointing unnervingly skywards in a totally different direction from the rest of her muzzle and face. Her schnoz is so mobile it reminds me of the nose of an anteater, which is ironic because when she is out in the garden that's exactly what she does! By contrast, when Tam sleeps he is just a picture of jowly scrummieness - a big teddy bear that you want to go and hug. Watching them in the evenings as they sleep was another reminder that these two really were such an odd couple.

TWENTY-ONE - Week 8

It might be easy to think that Maia was a wimpy little pointy nose and it is true, she would never win in a battle of strength with Tam. No, Maia is much more tactical. When she first arrived she wasn't very good at solving problems and working things out. She almost seemed - dare I say it - a little bit thick. When presented with a challenge she would just stand there looking a bit bemused. I started giving her games that involved problem solving. At first they were really basic such as throwing a bit of kibble on the floor for Maia to sniff out. Gradually I increased the difficulty by partially covering the kibble or putting it inside a small egg box where she would have to open the box to get to the goodies. Eventually I was able to put some kibble in a sealed cardboard tube and Maia had to work out how to get into the tube and eat the kibble. She seemed to enjoy the challenges but I was always careful to make sure they remained well within her limited capabilities. I didn't want her to get disheartened and give up. It was amazing how hard she found these simple little tasks. But that was then. How this little hound has changed. Nowadays if Maia is confronted with a problem, instead of immediately giving up she thinks things through and works it out. Turns out she's not quite so 'thick' after all.

The dogs were a bit bored so I gave them each a chew to keep them busy. Maia didn't waste any time eating hers, but Tam likes to savour his treats and still had some left after Maia had finished hers. Tam then made a very poor decision - he seized the chance to tease Maia. He decided in his wisdom to parade back and forth in front of her with the bit of his chew sticking out the side of his mouth. Big mistake! Once he was sure that she had seen it, he went out into the garden with Maia in hot pursuit. I followed them out. Tam doing his funny strutty walk, with head lowered, ears back and tail wagging as Maia trailed behind him staring longingly at his chew. Oh, the power! Tam knew that Maia would never be bold enough to take the chew out of his mouth and he was enjoying teasing her. Now Maia is not at all confrontational but she is sneaky. She waited while Tam had his fun knowing he would eventually drop his guard. It didn't take long. Something caught his attention so he went off to investigate. He placed the last little piece of his chew on the grass and the moment he did so it was stolen so fast he didn't even see her do it. Maia snatched the chew and made a quick getaway. Once Tam finished his sniffing he went to pick up his chew but it had gone. Poor Tam was still hunting for it long after Maia had settled back in the cottage and started chomping.

Tam learnt an important lesson that day - never underestimate his little sister. Maia, triumphant, ran back outside and another crazy zoomies session ensued.

There were clearly no bad feelings as that night Tam decided to sleep on the floor next to Maia's bed. When I woke they were laying head to head just inches apart. On second thoughts, maybe there were bad feelings and Tam was keeping a *really* close eye on her!

As Maia's confidence grew we started walking further along the bridle path. She was beginning to get used to seeing other people out and was starting to understand that they posed her no threat. In most encounters I was able to walk Maia back to a wider point on the track, tuck her over to one side, call Tam for moral support and wait for the walker to pass. I put myself between Maia and the approaching walker, crouched down to Maia's level and held her in my arms without restricting her. This allowed her to watch the walker from a safe distance without feeling threatened.

There were some regular walkers who Maia got to recognise. After she had seen them a few times she was OK with them standing a little closer to us while I caught up with village gossip. I had missed chatting to my fellow villagers on our walks and it was lovely to talk to them again instead of shouting 'hello' from a safe distance! Maia was fine as long as they ignored her. If they looked at her or talked to her, her anxiety sky-rocketed and she backed away and looked for an escape. She could cope with being in reasonable proximity to people, but she wasn't ready to interact with them yet.

Maia was getting used to seeing all sorts of different people on her walks. I always gave her lots of space and slowly her fear turned to curiosity. There were certainly some people she was more worried about than others and it was difficult to identify exactly why that was. It didn't seem to be related to age, build, clothing or hair colour. It must have been something less discernible such as their posture, gait or even their smell. I just had to trust her judgment and make sure that we always gave those individuals a wide berth.

Maia was definitely starting to respond differently. She was daring herself to put her trust in me to take control in scary situations. It was a huge leap of faith for Maia and a huge responsibility for me. If I ever made an error of judgment she would hold it against me forever. Maia NEVER forgets!

TWENTY-TWO - Month 3

Maia had been part of my family for three months and she was getting so much more confident around the home that I was making very few dispensations for her. In many ways she was just like a normal happy dog. Her main issue remained fear of people so I felt it was time to introduce her to some more visitors. I wanted to start with a familiar face so I asked Barb round again. It had been a couple of months since her last visit and I was keen to see how Maia would react this time.

Maia immediately recognised Barb and was clearly delighted to see her. She went straight up to Barb (a first), tail wagging (another first), jumped up on the sofa and stood waiting for Barb to join her (another first). As Barb was too busy with Tam, Maia impatiently got down from the sofa and went straight up to Barb again and insisted on some attention (another first). When Barb managed to break away from Tam she sat down on the sofa, Maia began a very thorough pointy nose information-gathering investigation. She sniffed Barb from her face right down to her feet - it was a great opportunity to learn all she could about Barb. Then Maia repeatedly poked Barb with her nose demanding to be stroked and then laid flat out on the floor by Barb's feet (yet another first). It was such a huge change from her usual reaction but showed that having our protocol in place had given Maia so much confidence that she was ready to start approaching visitors on her own terms. It was so wonderful to see her so excited and welcoming towards a visitor.

Maia lay at Barb's feet for the rest of her visit. This was significant as she was making herself extremely vulnerable. A bold decision, particularly from a hound with such a high level of self-preservation as Maia! She was so relaxed she didn't even make any attempt to get up when Barb went to leave. I could never have dreamt that Maia could have got to this point after just a few months. Happy days!

Seeing Maia's reaction to Barb gave me the confidence to push her boundaries a little further. After many months of declining performance I decided to bite the bullet and get my shower replaced. I had been putting it off for as long as I could as I was concerned how Maia would react to a tradesman in the cottage, but now as my shower was just a trickle I had little option but to get it done.

Up to this point, all visitors had behaved the same way but this visit would be very different. I arranged for the plumber to come in

133

through the back door so he didn't have to walk past Maia in the living room. I also closed the glass door between the living room and the kitchen so Maia could watch him from a safe distance without feeling threatened. All I could do now was cross my fingers and hope that she coped.

When the plumber arrived, both dogs stood by the glass door with excited anticipation. When Maia first saw him she took a few steps back but quickly returned to her original vantage point. She watched as he brought his kit in and made his way to the bathroom. I was thrilled with her initial response as I had expected her to stand behind Tam while keeping a nervous eye on the plumber. Instead she was standing right alongside Tam, nose pressed against the kitchen door leaving a lovely nose smear on the glass.

Tam was extremely excited when he saw the plumber. As he was stuck behind the kitchen door he started to get frustrated. He has always struggled to cope with frustration. If he had a problem with something he was always quick to let me know - and believe me, he didn't hold back. Today was no different. Tam started barking in a desperate attempt to get noticed. Luckily for Tam, the plumber loved dogs and was keen to meet him so I let a delighted Tam through to say 'hello'. As soon as I opened the door, Tam burst through like a bulldozer and sat in front of the plumber, staring into his eyes relishing the attention. He was intent on taking full advantage of the opportunity. After they had exchanged greetings Tam returned to the living room much to Maia's delight. She didn't seem particularly worried about the plumber but was definitely happier with her bodyguard at her side.

Maia watched the plumber working for a short time but quickly got bored with it all, climbed on to the sofa and fell asleep. She stayed like that the whole time the plumber was working. I hoped she was taking it all in subliminally because it looked like she wasn't going to remember much of this visit. Tam remained by the kitchen door ever hopeful for another opportunity to get some more attention.

About an hour later the job was done. As I went to admire my shiny new shower I let Tam through to say his goodbyes. Maia barely lifted an eyelid. Far from being worried by the plumber, she couldn't even be bothered to get up off the sofa and watch him when he packed up and left. The plumber's visit couldn't have gone better and was a good precursor for future visitors to the cottage. That is assuming that Maia remembered any of his visit having just slept through it all!

By now it was mid-summer and the weather was scorching hot. Tam insisted on sunbathing in the direct sunlight despite there being loads of shade available so I had to keep hosing him down with cold water which he loved. Maia watched on and was quite perplexed. Was Tam out of his mind? After being hosed down Tam always shook off the excess water. Unfortunately, Maia was usually caught in the spray zone and was unimpressed. She may only have been caught by a few drops of very fine spray but that was enough to make her squint her eyes and walk away in disgust. Once she was a safe distance she had a good shake. Such an over-reaction. More evidence that she was starting to develop Diva tendencies.

Downstairs in the cottage is always lovely and cool, which is great in August but not quite so great in February. It provides a welcome escape from the heat but it can still get very hot upstairs, especially at night. In order to try and keep Tam cool I decided that we would all sleep downstairs that night. The last time I had slept downstairs was on Maia's first night when she had been terrified of the bedding and too scared to venture far from the sofa. It would be very interesting to see her reaction now.

As I gathered up my bedding and brought it downstairs Maia was keen to come and investigate, excitedly circling it as I put it all down on the floor. I went into the kitchen to grab my glass of water and when I returned barely two seconds later, she was curled up in the middle of my duvet looking very pleased with herself. I have to hand it to her, it was a very quick manoeuvre but having spent the last ten weeks sitting on the floor while Maia hogged the sofa, I wasn't going to give up my bed quite so readily. I asked Maia to get off my duvet and must have accidentally tripped her turbo-boost button as she went berserk! She took off round the room in zoomies mode then circled round behind me. As I looked round at her she whacked me with both of her front legs in her karate chop move that she had been perfecting. Her claw caught me just below my eye. That was close! She was way too excited to calm down. As I protected my face she continued to pummel my back and goodness it was painful. Who would think those long skinny delicate legs could pack such a whack! I looked at the grin on her face and the manic look in her eyes, she was having a great time.

It was no good I had to call in back up. He stepped in heroically. I moved to the side and Tam took my place. Blows rained down on him but he barely felt it though his padding. He rolled onto his side and started aimlessly swiping and air-snapping back at Maia. This was right up Tam's street. He was delighted that Maia was being such an enthusiastic opponent. A few more swipes and it was all over, Maia had a shake-down so Tam mirrored her. It had been a lovely game and had ended by mutual agreement instead of the usual scenario where Maia takes offence and abruptly ends it.

This wasn't the gentle wind-down to bed time I had anticipated but it had been amazing seeing Tam and Maia playing rough - well Maia was playing rough while Tam showed enormous restraint! As I got into my makeshift bed, Maia made herself comfortable on the sofa with Tam lying on the floor next to us. Time to sleep.

In the morning, I am not sure exactly what hit me but as I peered up through bleary eyes I could see the outline of Maia's bat-like ears standing over me so I had a pretty good idea! Then I saw her over-excited eyes and then her pointy nose coming towards my face at great speed for one poke and then another. I could just about make out Tam standing next to her, ears pricked looking down at me with a silly look on his face. I am sure they thought this one up between them. I guess that meant that it was time to get up.

I had barely got out of my makeshift bed when quick as a flash Maia was back curled up in the middle of it, pointy nose resting on her front legs looking up at me with laughing eyes. She knew that she wasn't really allowed on the bed but she had done it in such good humour that I let her enjoy her moment. This shy timid little hound had definitely changed and was becoming a cheeky little princess.

Maia wasn't the only one with cheeky tendencies. Tam has a very cheeky yet endearing habit of stealing socks from my clothes airer. He then comes over and slowly struts past me with his tail wagging furiously and the sweetest look on his face. He finds it absolutely hilarious and I have to admit to encouraging this blatant theft as it is so funny to watch. He knows that it is a dead cert if he wants to get my attention and he *really* plays to the gallery. In all the years he has been playing this game, he has always given up my socks as soon as I have asked for them and apart from being a bit soggy, he has never damaged them. But that was in the pre-Maia days. Now this game plays out slightly differently.

It always starts the same way with Tam stealing the sock off the rack and strutting around the living room but then it takes a turn for the worse - for my socks anyway - because that's when Maia joins in. Unlike Tam, Maia isn't quite so gentle with textiles. On this occasion Maia was able to grab the loose end of the sock in Tam's mouth and have a tug of war. Sadly, I was upstairs so I didn't hear the threads in my sock tearing under the tension. If I had seen this game, I would have jumped in and reclaimed the sock. However, in my absence, Tam and Maia were free to continue. If Maia had given up first, my sock would have lived to see another day. But Tam must have let go first, leaving my sock at Maia's mercy. She took it to a quiet corner of the room and nibbled at it until there was a hole in it just large enough to make it unwearable. At that point her work was done and she discarded the sock and returned to the sofa. I happened across the soggy, stretched and nibbled sock some time later. Another one bites the dust.

Maia's confidence continued to grow, so it was time for her to meet her new grandparents. It was going to be quite a test as up to this point I had only had individual visitors. Two people would be a much bigger challenge. To add to this, my lovely father is quite tall and has a big booming voice. Knowing Maia's fear of men we were going to have to play this one very carefully.

I set up a chair for my father, away from the sofa, the night before so that Maia had plenty of time to examine it before my parents arrived. Unfortunately, that chair also signalled to Tam that we were having visitors which meant that he would be up bright and early and would be *very* excited.

My father was under strict instructions during his visit to keep as far away from Maia as possible and to completely ignore her. Tam LOVES his grandad and always throws himself at him so I didn't think it would be too much of a challenge for my father to ignore Maia. He would be far too busy wrestling with Tam.

I arranged for my mother to come in first to give Maia time to settle. When she was calm I would invite my father in. He was quite happy to wait in the car reading his book until he was summoned. The first part of the plan worked well. My mother came in and sat down like all previous visitors and almost immediately Maia was up on the sofa next to her. I felt it was time for my father to make his grand entrance! He made his way down the steps and walked into the cottage. As expected, the moment Maia saw him she was off the sofa and into her den. I was confident that she would return to the sofa at some stage during the visit but that decision was entirely down to Maia. There was no pressure for her to do anything she wasn't comfortable with. After rugby tackling Tam my father was able to make it to his chair where Tam continued to entertain him.

Maia hid in her den and watched his every move very closely but she had managed to hold her nerve and stay in the same room which was really encouraging.

I chatted with my parents for a while before Maia regained enough courage to climb back up onto the sofa. She was very tense, curled up in a tight ball, eyes like saucers and she wouldn't take them off my father. I sat on the floor next to Maia and reassured her. Despite her obvious tension she was doing remarkably well, sharing the sofa with my mother and just a few metres from my father.

My father did a great job ignoring her. I don't think he so much as glanced at her the whole time he was here. The only time she got really worried was when either of my parents stood up and walked around the cottage. This was understandable as the cottage is very small so it feels quite crowded with three adults and two large-ish dogs in it. I also hadn't taught Maia to cope with visitors moving around the cottage yet. Maia was now reasonably comfortable with visitors coming in and sitting down and getting up and leaving. The next stage would be to get her used to them moving around. With two visitors today it wasn't the right time to tackle this as Maia was understandably more anxious. I would wait until the next time I had a single visitor and would continue her training then. Despite her initial fears, it was encouraging to see that she quickly settled as soon as my visitors made it back to their seats. She was watching and learning the whole time.

My parents stayed for a few hours and we had a lovely catch up. After a while Maia started to relax and even asked my mother to stroke her as we continued to natter. Eventually she dropped her guard and fell asleep. I couldn't have wished for a better outcome. Not only had Maia coped with having two visitors in the cottage, but one of them was a very manly man sitting only a few metres away! Maia had risen to the challenge. What a really lovely day.

Golden retrievers are known for having 'soft mouths' which means they can carry fragile things really gently without damaging them. It is a very important trait in working retrievers as they are trained to pick up game such as pheasants without damaging them. Tam is no exception. He is so gentle with his soft toys that he still has some of the same toys he had when a puppy nearly six years ago.

Tam likes to have a big soft toy in his mouth most of the time. It is a comfort to him and something that he is driven to do. Sometimes visitors to the cottage misinterpret this gesture and when Tam walks up to them with a toy they try to take it from him. He will always give his toy if anyone tries to take it whether he wants to or not, so I have to ask guests not to take Tam's toy unless he drops it for them. Unfortunately I can't explain this to Maia.

Luckily Tam and Maia usually go for different toys, which is good as Tam would be absolutely devastated if Maia destroyed any of his favourites. Tam likes the really soft, pink and brightly coloured ones - they are very much in keeping with his gentle personality. Maia tends to go for the firmer dark brown furry ones that more closely resemble bunnies. Since she arrived I had encouraged them to stick to their own toys. This meant Tam would always be able to grab some of his toys if he needed them for comfort and Maia had an outlet for her more destructive tendencies. Generally it worked pretty well however when Maia was feeling playful all Tam's toys became fair game.

It was a lovely afternoon so we all went out into the garden. As Tam ambled down the garden, Maia raced up behind him and as she passed him at speed she tried to snatch his toy from his mouth. Whilst she came close, she didn't quite succeed. This was quite a shock for me and for Tam. Maia was still very respectful of him so it was a bold gesture, even in play! Maia was in determined mood and not ready to give up. After another couple of high speed laps round the garden she had another go. As before, she raced up behind Tam and made another grab at his toy. This time she was able to knock it out of his mouth but she dropped it as she made her getaway. Would she have the audacity to have another attempt? Of course she would, but this time Tam was ready for her. As Maia ran up behind him, Tam tightened his grip on his toy and turned his head away from her. It worked. Maia accepted defeat and came to a halt, puffing hard. Tam might have won that battle but it only a matter of time before Maia had perfected the art of blatant daylight robbery.

Tam changed forever that day. My lovely pedigree golden retriever with his super soft mouth would never be quite the same again. Whenever Maia was around he would hold onto his toys with a slightly firmer grip. Goodbye lovely soft mouth.

Karen from Forever Hounds trust called me to let me know she was in the area and wondered if she could pop in to see Maia. I was delighted. Maia had come on so much I was keen to show her off. After all Karen had done to help introduce Tam and me to Maia, it would be a joy to see her again. Unfortunately things didn't quite go according to plan ...

Karen arrived about an hour later. Tam gave Karen his usual greeting but I noticed immediately that Maia wasn't behaving quite the way she had with other visitors. She ran to her den and looked quite uneasy. It was really unexpected and sadly set the tone for the rest of the visit. Karen sat down on the sofa and after a short time Maia climbed up and joined her but Maia remained very tense and uneasy.

I wanted to show Karen that all her time, dedication and commitment to Maia while she had been in the charity's care had paid off. I wanted her to see a happy and relaxed Maia and perhaps even get a taste of her cheeky side with a little nose poke, but it soon became clear this wasn't going to happen this time. Karen was so kind and understanding but it was clear she shared my disappointment.

I think there were two reasons why this visit went the way it did. Usually when I have visitors to my home we have a lot more time. I felt right from the start that I had placed Maia under too much pressure. As Karen had come specifically to see Maia it was difficult to follow the usual three rules. There was definitely pressure to engage Maia faster than she was comfortable with.

It is also possible that when Maia saw Karen it triggered memories from her previous life in kennels. She might even have thought that Karen was here to take her away again. Whatever the reason, I felt that I had really let Maia down.

It became clear that evening that Maia had been quite shaken by the visit. She was generally withdrawn and she licked and nibbled at herself for most of the evening. A stark reminder that although Maia had made remarkable progress, she was still vulnerable to certain triggers. I gave her some healing and she quickly fell asleep and didn't wake for the rest of the evening.

I would love to invite Karen back when she has lots of time to take things really slowly with Maia but as Karen spends every spare minute helping hounds in need, her time is at a premium. Whether Karen would want to come and see us again is another matter!

Over the weeks there had been a huge change in Maia's attitude. Increased bravery and curiosity meant that things she used to find frightening, she now found absolutely fascinating. In light of her recent progress I felt it was time for her to face an old adversary, cardboard boxes!

Despite being Tam's favourite game, he had been deprived the opportunity to shred large boxes for some time due to Maia's sensitivities. The last time he'd had a large box to destroy was the day when Maia had her complete meltdown and I hadn't indulged him since. Quite a few smaller boxes had met their fate at his paws recently, but none of the extra-large boxes that Tam *really* loved. However, all that was about to change. I placed a new food order so very soon there would be several extra-large boxes just waiting to be torn into tiny little pieces by my crazed golden retriever. But how would Maia react?

When the delivery arrived Tam could hardly contain his delight. I kept a close eye on Maia as I unpacked the boxes and she seemed to be coping OK so I gave one of the boxes to Tam. In an instant he attacked it frantically scratching at the box with his claws and tearing it with his teeth. Maia watched on warily but she remained in the same room, which was a massive improvement on the previous occasion. Tam continued to trash the box and Maia looked on, watching his every move. He was having such a great time but she really couldn't quite understand why.

It wasn't long before Tam had done a great job of breaking down the box into tiny little pieces. As he lay on a carpet of shredded cardboard, panting after all his exertions with a huge satisfied grin on his face, curiosity finally got the better of Maia. In a moment of overwhelming bravery she summoned up all her courage, leant forward and snatched a little piece of cardboard. She rushed over to the only corner of the living room that didn't have shredded cardboard on the floor and set about destroying her own piece. What a change from her reaction just a few months earlier. Tam went to have a drink which gave Maia an opportunity to go over and examine the devastation he had left behind. At least I had enjoyed a cardboard-free home for a few weeks. Normality had returned.

From that day on, whenever Tam had a box to shred Maia always insisted on having a little piece of her own to tear. She progressed to shredding ever larger pieces with increasing vigour. Tam had taught her well. After several months her confidence developed so much that she even dared to have a nibble at the remains of a large box that Tam had just decimated. The box was bigger than she was.

Maia much preferred shredding paper to cardboard. Any letters or documents or even boxes of tissues were fair game. She was very quick. I only had to turn my back for a second and that was enough time for Maia to strike. When I looked back moments later she would be lying in a little circle of shredded paper with the sweetest, most innocent look on her face. Who, me? On a positive note, I had been considering upgrading my paper shredder but thanks to Maia it no longer seemed necessary.

Overcoming fear of cardboard boxes

TWENTY-THREE ~ Month 4

Four months in and Maia continued to amaze me with her development. Not only did she look like a totally different dog with her sleek shiny coat, confident posture and muscular physique, but there had been a profound shift in her overall attitude over the last couple of weeks. It was almost like someone had flicked a switch. Her level of trust had skyrocketed along with her confidence. She was now really affectionate and playful - both Tam and I bear the scars to show for it - and she was such a happy little soul.

She was also getting so much better walking on the lead. As she gained so much in confidence she wanted to go off and explore, to deviate from the main pathways and be able to join Tam 'up front'. She longed to check out those tantalising smells but it was almost impossible for her to do so with me in tow just a couple of metres behind. I decided that Maia was ready to swap her usual lead for a 10 metre long line.

Long lines have to be introduced carefully by gradually letting them out so the dog learns how much extra space they have. They should always be attached to a harness, never a collar, to reduce the risk of injury should the dog suddenly run to the end of the line at speed. They take a bit of getting used to but they are a safer, more reliable alternative to extendable leads. The long line gave Maia far more freedom. She could stop for sniffs and even have a bit of a run and she clearly enjoyed the extra independence. Tam was a little less thrilled. He had been enjoying his walks free from harassment from his weird little sister. He could take his time and do as he pleased without Maia cramping his style. Unfortunately for Tam, if he was now within a 10 metre radius of me, he invariably had company.

Tam had always been an incredible role model for Maia, giving her confidence and showing her the ropes. That was until today when he well and truly blotted his copybook. We were having a lovely walk across the fields. Maia was on the long line and Tam off lead. Tam had run ahead and was deeply engrossed in a smell when I saw his nemesis approaching. Buddy is a lovely Jack Russell terrier but unfortunately he has had a grudge match going with Tam for more than five years. Buddy can be quite reactive towards other dogs and sadly when Tam was just a young dog, Buddy ran over and attacked him. Tam never forgot it and since that day became frightened of Buddy. While it is understandable, I worked hard to make sure this behaviour didn't escalate. I always put Tam on the lead whenever we saw Buddy, allowed lots of extra space when we passed and gave him lots of praise when he was calm around Buddy to build his confidence.

It is very common when dogs get frightened in a dog attack that their fear can make them reactive towards other dogs - even if they have never shown any aggression in the past. Tam's fear of the breed was intensified when he was set upon by a different Jack Russell just a week after Buddy's attack. That one pinned Tam to the ground by his ear and Tam was screaming in terror. It took me over a minute to get the terrier to release its grip on him and it was a really traumatic experience. Don't scoff - Tam might be four times the size of a Jack Russell but those little guys can be tough!

Sadly, in dog on dog attacks the emotional scars often take much longer to heal that the physical wounds. Many reactive dogs only became that way after they have been attacked. Fear makes them quicker to react aggressively to other dogs if they feel threatened. Sometimes it only takes one bad incident to trigger a lifelong issue of dog-directed fear aggression.

It can also be extremely distressing for owners. Seeing Tam being attacked was devastating. It can cause a great deal of anxiety after the event which can greatly impact the enjoyment owners get from walking their dog. So, if a dog has a known history of aggression it is vital to keep them on a lead around other dogs, and give other dogs a wide berth to prevent them triggering a lifelong fear issue.

As we continued across the field Buddy's owner spotted us. Since the attack he always put Buddy on a lead when he saw Tam. I called Tam to me but as I did so, he spotted Buddy and stopped in his tracks. I called Tam again and he looked at me and then looked back at Buddy, back to me then back to Buddy. He was clearly torn. Go to Lisa for treats and praise or seeing that Buddy was on his lead, go and bait him. After much deliberation, Tam chose to ignore me and ran towards Buddy. He stopped short and started barking at him. Buddy retaliated with all guns blazing but he couldn't reach Tam. After a few seconds, Tam felt he had put Buddy in his place and ran back to me as if nothing had happened.

The only positive to come out of this sorry tale was that Maia didn't seem the least bit concerned about the boys having a stand-off. She didn't even seem concerned when I called Tam from across the field at the top of my voice. The only concern she had was the length of time it took me to put my hand in my pocket and give her another treat.

I had been dreading having to take Maia to the vet. Vet surgeries can be such scary places for dogs. It can be frightening enough for us humans when we have to go to the doctors but at least we have a pretty good idea why we are there and what's going to happen to us. It must be far worse for our dogs. They have no idea why they are there or what will happen to them. Vet surgeries are often quite compact spaces full of strange and unfamiliar smells, funny noises and scary equipment. Unfamiliar people try to conduct often unpleasant and invasive procedures against the dog's will and if the dog tries to object they are restrained. They might have had a previous bad experience at a vet practice, and if all that wasn't enough, they are often surrounded by lots of equally fearful dogs.

For a fearful dog like Maia, this must be absolutely terrifying. She was still so fearful of strangers, I was really worried about what impact a vet visit would have on her. I was about to find out.

We had just returned from a lovely walk in the secure dog field when I noticed that Maia was a bit lame on her right front leg. It didn't come as a complete surprise as she'd had a really good run. She could easily have hurt herself while she was racing round or she might even have jarred herself as she jumped out of the car. She looked like she had pulled a muscle in her shoulder so I decided to rest her for a couple of days and then see how she was. Resting dogs can be quite a challenge especially if they feel well in themselves but I didn't think it would be too much of a problem with my super lazy lurcher.

The following morning Maia seemed really quite lame so I felt that I had no option. I rang the Vet and explained that Maia was really fearful so examination might be difficult. I requested that we have an appointment when the surgery was likely to be at its quietest and I arranged for Maia to stay in the car until she was ready to be seen to avoid her having to hang around in the waiting room. Of course Tam would be coming along too for moral support.

When we arrived I was able to take Maia and Tam straight through the waiting area into the consultation room. Maia was absolutely terrified. I could see the panic in her huge eyes darting to the right then to the left and it was easy to see from her body language just how scared she was. We were greeted by a lovely vet. We talked briefly and then she went to approach Maia but Tam sat down and blocked her way. He looked up at her a big grin on his face wagging his tail. There was no way she was getting to Maia without saying hello to him first. Tam was always quick to introduce himself to the vets, even if all they had ever done to him was stick needles in him and put their fingers where frankly he would rather they didn't!

After giving Tam a quick cuddle the vet made her way to Maia who had squashed herself against the wall in the corner. The vet offered a treat but she was far too scared to take it. She then crouched down to give Maia a gentle stroke but every touch just added to Maia's fear. Dogs like Tam get reassurance from human touch but for Maia it just added to her terror. As the vet stood up and started to question me over Maia's symptoms, Tam stood very close to Maia to reassure her. It was moving to watch. Tam was still far better at helping Maia through her fear than me.

After a few minutes, it was time for the vet to examine Maia. As expected she completely froze. I felt so helpless. I knew that all I could do was send healing and leave it to Tam to support her. As the vet checked Maia over, Tam put his huge head between the vet and Maia's face. He did so in a gentle yet protective manner. The vet tried to manipulate Maia's leg but by this time she had shut down. There was no way that she would be able to indicate pain as she was rigid with tension. There was no obvious swelling or heat so the vet agreed it was probably a shoulder injury but as Maia was so scared there wasn't much more she could do without further investigation. We agreed that for now it would be in Maia's best interests if she was sent home with pain relief for some rest.

Tam remained close to Maia for the entire time. As the consultation drew to a close, he said his goodbyes to the vet and led the way back out to the car. As soon as Maia left the surgery, the life started to return to her. She had a big shake-down to release all her pent up tension and she seemed much brighter. During the drive home, I kept replaying Tam's behaviour in my mind. It was yet another humbling reminder about how connected animals are.

After a couple of weeks' rest I was able to build Maia's exercise up again and she hasn't had any further recurrence of her leg injury.

As the nights started to draw in, it was getting harder to find a place for Maia to have a good safe off-lead run. The secure dog field had been fabulous to get us through the summer but as the days were getting shorter, there were fewer available slots. Maia had been coping incredibly well with her lead walks but it was clear that as she was fitter and more confident her weekly off-lead runs weren't enough. After a few days of lead walks she started to get quite strong again and her frustration was clear. She really needed the opportunity to have a good run more than once a week.

I was running out of options, when out of the blue I had the most wonderful offer from a good friend of mine, Maureen. She had a three acre field that had been previously used for horses but was now lying empty and she offered it to me as a safe place to walk Tam and Maia. It had post and rail fencing with sheep wire running all the way round the perimeter. The fence was lower than the dog-walking field but I didn't feel it would be an issue. Maia had great recall and it was only her fear of people that would make her bolt. The best thing of all was that the field was just a mile from my cottage which meant that we could go there every day.

Our first visit was wonderful. It was another gloriously sunny day. I walked the dogs round the field so they knew where the boundary fence was and then I let Tam off. I continued to keep Maia on lead until she was a little less excited and then quietly unclipped her lead. It took a few seconds for her to realise that she was free and then she took off like a rocket. She looked amazing sprinting round the whole field three times before collapsing in a happy heap right next to me, gasping for air and desperately trying to get her breath back. Tam managed about a quarter of a lap before going into sniff and mark mode. Well at least he had made a bit of an effort.

The other great benefit was that it ran alongside a lane which was regularly used by walkers. Maia would have a great opportunity to people-watch from behind the safety of the fence. It would let her get as close as she felt comfortable to all sorts of people and dogs of all shapes and sizes. I knew if Tam spotted anyone he would be at the fence like a shot so Maia would be able to take his lead.

There was a fence running down the middle of the field, dividing it into two with gaps at each end. It was easy to just climb through the fence and let the dogs run underneath. Well, when I say 'dogs' I meant Tam. Maia couldn't work it out at all! I climbed through the fence, called the dogs and Tam came over, ducked under the fence and joined me. Maia ran up to the fence and stood on the other side as if it was a three metre wall! After a great deal of consideration Maia suddenly took off in full flight. What was she doing? She sprinted all the way up the field, skidded through the gap at the top and then raced back to where Tam and I were. Despite covering a distance of about 300 metres it took her seconds. It was several weeks before Maia understood that she could duck under but she still preferred the gaps. I think it was an excuse for an extra sprint!

To help build Maia's confidence with people I invited Dan round again. It had been a couple of months since his first visit and she'd had lots of positive experiences since then. I hoped Dan might get to see a bit of her cheeky personality this time. Maia wasn't the only one who would benefit from a visit from Dan. Tam needed a bit of rough and tumble and there was no better opponent.

The difference in Maia's attitude was clear from the moment Dan arrived. While Tam monopolised him, Maia wasted little time in resuming her position on the sofa. She barely reacted at all when Dan sat down next to her and it wasn't long before she was poking him for strokes. Her attitude was amazing.

Dan and I chatted for a while then I felt it was time to take Maia to the field for a run. It was the first time I had invited anyone to join us and it would be interesting to see how she would cope away from the security of the cottage. I asked Dan to wait while I put Tam and Maia in the car. Once they were safely strapped in Dan came up to join us. Maia initially looked a bit worried as Dan opened the door and sat down but the excitement and anticipation of a run was far greater than her slight uncertainty about Dan.

Once we arrived at the field gate, Dan waited in the car until the dogs were safely in the field and then he came to join us. Maia soon forgot her fear and after several high speed laps of the field she joined us as we all walked round the field together. Maia wanted to play so I asked Dan to run away from her. As expected it triggered her chase response and she started running after Dan around the field. It was wonderful to see her actually running *towards* Dan. Of course it wasn't long before she had caught up with him so she did a couple of zoomie circuits before chasing him again. Timeout! I'm not sure who needed a break more, Maia - who always gets very out of puff after running in zoomies mode - or Dan who'd had a huge workload recently and hadn't had an opportunity for much physical exercise. It was quite amusing watching the two of them puffing away as they both tried to catch their breath but they looked like they'd had a great time.

Once they had recovered, they set off again. This time Dan turned to chase Maia. She immediately ran away at top speed, but moments later she circled and ran right up to him again. It was wonderful to watch. The only slight problem was that Tam also loved playing chase with Dan. As Dan ran round the field with Maia, he was also trying to dodge Tam, who by this time was way too excited for his own good, careering around in full wrecking ball mode. It was such a chaotic scene. Seeing Tam gallop towards me whilst looking in the opposite direction sent some interesting thoughts flashing through my mind. Was my personal accident insurance up to date? How would I work if Tam incapacitated me? How would I be able to walk them with both my legs in traction? Luckily apart from a couple of glancing blows where I nearly got out of the way in time, we all remained in one piece. Spirits were running high as we drove home.

Within minutes of arriving home Maia had crashed out on the sofa, Tam was fast asleep on the floor next to her and it wasn't long before Dan was snoozing on the sofa with them. It gave me the chance to reflect. It had been so wonderful seeing Maia chasing Dan around the field with Tam doing his best to keep up. They were having such a great time but I think that I was having the best time of all. Seeing Maia's confidence escalating to that point had been thrilling. It was such a milestone in her rehab and I also had some video footage to record the moment for posterity! All I had to do now was arrange more play dates for Maia so she could form positive associations with as many people as possible.

After about an hour I woke Dan, plied him with lots of strong coffee and sent him on his long journey home. I didn't hear much from the dogs that evening. They woke briefly to eat their supper then they both crashed out again until it was time for bed. It's fair to say that they were very happy dogs!

TWENTY-FOUR - Month 5

Like many sighthounds, Maia has a very thin sleek coat on her back and sides and almost no hair at all on her belly which makes her very susceptible to feeling the cold. As the temperature started to drop I had to make sure that she had some comfortable coats to ensure that she stayed warm and cosy. There was just one small issue. When Maia was in kennels she had a reputation for removing and chewing coats to the point that they were unable to leave a coat on her. This could be a bit of a problem as my little old cottage didn't have any central heating and got quite chilly. Maia would definitely need to wear a coat to keep warm. Forever Hounds Trust made sure that Maia had a heat lamp in her kennel so she could keep warm without having to wear a coat. Now I love that little lurcher to the moon and back but I had no intention of making a heat lamp a feature in my living room! Somehow I had to show her that coats were better when they were wrapped around her body rather than shredded into tiny pieces strewn all over the floor.

The dog coats I had in mind for Maia were lovely soft fleece coats that were warm and super comfortable but sadly didn't have an indestructible outer. Teaching Maia not to destroy her clothes could get expensive. I started to introduce her to the coat very slowly. It would have been easy to just put it on and leave her to get used to it but Maia already had a pretty dim view of coats. I wanted her to accept and consent to wearing a coat so she would be less inclined to remove it!

I laid Maia's coat on the sofa so she could have a really good look at it before I tried to put it on. As she inspected it I gave her loads of praise to help her learn that coats were good. The next step was to gently lay the coat over her back so she could get used to the feel of it covering her without it restricting her. As soon as she felt the coat on her back she jumped but she quickly relaxed. After a few seconds I took the coat off and gave her loads of praise and repeated the process. After several repetitions Maia accepted the coat and seemed happy with it lying over her back. I felt that she was ready to move onto the next stage. Some dogs can be sensitive to the sound of the clips opening or closing. I moved away from her to check her reaction when I clicked the clip closed. She didn't seem to mind but she was still sensitive to physical touch and jumped every time the coat touched her. It was possible that she had some pain or discomfort in her back that caused this hyper-sensitivity but it seemed more like the anticipation of something touching her that caused her to be tense. If her sensitivity persisted, I would get her checked out.

I gently placed the coat on Maia again, carefully fastened the chest strap and watched her closely for her reaction. She seemed happy with it so I took it off and repeated this step leaving the coat on her for a little longer each time. The final stage was to do up the belly strap. Again, Maia didn't seem to react. Great. Coat training done. Now all I had to do was to convince her not to eat them!

It wasn't long before the temperature plummeted and Maia's coat training was put to the test. Right from the start she seemed very comfortable wearing it. She never made any attempt to nibble it so ever the optimist I hoped it had been the boredom of kennels that caused her to shred them.

The day arrived when it was cold enough to have to leave Maia's coat on when I went out to work in the morning. As I closed the door behind me I wondered how much of it would still be attached to her when I returned home a couple of hours later.

When I returned home I got a lovely welcome but I noticed a small nibbled area on the neck of Maia's coat. It was just a small patch, but I had a horrible feeling that whenever Maia caught sight of it, she would be compelled to nibble at it again.

As I was sitting with Maia a little later, I noticed that she started to fiddle with the nibbled area. It was actually quite good that she had begun nibbling right in front of me as it gave me an opportunity to correct her. She clearly didn't know that it was 'wrong' so I quietly gave her an 'a-aa'. Maia immediately stopped nibbling and looked up at me with her huge innocent eyes so I gave her loads of praise.

Watching Maia I could see that she was really thinking about what had happened. She resisted the temptation to have another nibble which showed great self-control but I would have to cover over the nibbled area as it was in her sight line and so impossible to resist. I had to make it as easy as possible for Maia to do the right thing.

I did a shockingly bad repair job, but at least it didn't look quite so tantalising, and it did the job. Maia never chewed that coat again. She had a slight nibble at one other coat once but that was it. It was almost as though she realised that coats did actually have a use. All I had to do after that day was hold her coat up and she would trot across the room and automatically put her head through the neck hole. Coats, sorted!

It wasn't long before Maia would be grateful for her coats as the weather took a turn for the worse. After enjoying quite a long dry spell, the heavens opened and the rain absolutely poured down. I waited for it to ease but it was unrelenting. We had to venture out at some stage so I took the plunge and got the dogs ready, decking out Maia in her lovely warm waterproofs. The dogs were doing their usual excited dance around the living room, I clipped on their leads and the anticipation built - until I opened the front door.

Tam was out the door in a flash. Maia on the other hand stood in the porch and looked devastated. Her whole demeanour changed in an instant and it would take a lot more convincing that this was a good idea. After doing a frankly epic job of encouraging Maia to step outside and get into the car, we set off to the field.

Tam couldn't have been happier. He was always in his element when it rained. Even when the rain was horizontal. Watching him trotting across the field head held high and tail held aloft he didn't have a care in the world. Maia looked a picture of misery. Eyes squinting, ears pinned back, head held low. After five minutes she had barely moved at all despite plenty of encouragement so I put her back in the car. She had a shake then stretched out on the back seat and fell asleep while Tam enjoyed another half hour playing in

The mud monster and the fair weather hound on a rainy day

the pouring rain. It was yet another example of how different these two were - although I was definitely with Maia on this one!

As Maia's confidence was growing she was starting to get a wincey bit cocky. She loved trips to the field so long as it wasn't raining, but as she was getting fitter and stronger she was starting to take risks. These involved cornering at breakneck speed with her body tilting at an alarming angle. I don't know how she managed to stay on her feet. Or I should say, *usually* managed to stay on her feet.

On this particular occasion Maia was incredibly full of herself, bouncing around the field trying to goad Tam into joining her for a game. Tam was far too busy catching up on all the new scents so Maia took matters into her own paws. She took off at top speed, zooming round in an over-excited frenzy. She had a tendency to criss-cross just in front of Tam mid zoomie, skimming past his nose. It was a manoeuvre that the Red Arrows would be proud of. Tam had come to accept that at some stage on our walk he was going to be harassed by a turbo charged pointy nosed blur and had learnt to ignore it. Unfortunately, Maia made an error of judgement. Tam and Maia impacted with some intensity. Maia flew through the air and flipped a full 360° - twice! Legs flailing, twisting around like a rag doll, it was horrendous. Everything seemed to happen in slow motion giving me enough time to think of all the potential fractures she could have inflicted on herself. When her fragile body finally came to rest lying flat-out and motionless in the grass my heart was in my mouth.

After what must only have been a couple of seconds - but felt like a lifetime - Maia got up, had a good shake and carried on as if nothing had happened.

I think I aged 10 years in those seconds. I will never forget the feeling of helplessness as I watched events unfold, As for Tam, I honestly don't think that he felt the impact. He didn't react if he had. He just went about his business in blissful ignorance.

Thankfully these crashes are a fairly rare occurrence and Maia seems to come out of them ... no, I'm not going to say it. I'm just going to go and touch some wood!

A couple of weeks had passed and it was time for another test for Maia. I decided to update my broadband and had arranged for an engineer to come round and install it. All the necessary kit was in my living room so it was going to be quite a challenge for Maia but I felt that she was ready for it.

The day arrived. I had already briefed the engineer about Maia. He seemed very pleasant on the phone and I was pretty confident that all would be fine. When he arrived I watched in horror as an incredibly tall man got out of the van. I wasn't just concerned for Maia. My cottage has really low ceilings so there was no way he would be able to stand up straight. As he came in, I warned him to mind his head. Tam was doing his friendly greeting while Maia eyed him suspiciously from the kitchen. The engineer went to his van to collect his kit and Maia returned to the sofa. He returned holding a very large holdall full of kit, a smaller bag and rolls of cable. Maia watched him very closely from the sofa.

The engineer was here for a couple of hours. He drilled, hammered and flicked pieces of cable around and Maia barely flinched. Then to my amazement, she got bored of watching him and fell asleep.

Maia was magnificent! I was so proud of her. We had an extremely tall - albeit very friendly - male stranger in the cottage making loads of noise and sudden movements just a few metres away from where she was lying yet she didn't seem to mind a bit. It was only a few months ago that she would panic and bolt if she saw anyone from over 200 metres away.

It was another significant breakthrough in her rehab and she really was going from strength to strength.

Mistimed zoomies

TWENTY-FIVE - Month 6

It was now six months since Maia arrived and I noticed yet another huge leap in her (now, over-) confidence. She was starting to get *really* cocky. She had definitely found her feet and I was seeing her real character shining through. She was nosey and wanted to be the first to know about *everything*. If anyone walked along the lane past the field, Maia was there like a rocket having a good look to see who it was. In the early days she would wait for Tam to go first but not anymore. He was far too slow and Maia wasn't prepared to wait. She also found her voice - literally. She often played with Riley the spaniel through the gate. She loved these games as he is super friendly and has so much energy - unlike the slow, boring Tam! I was watching them one afternoon as they ran up and down the garden together. Maia was getting increasingly excited - spinning and play-bowing. Finally, as they skidded to a halt by the fence I heard a 'woof!' It definitely wasn't Tam and it didn't sound like Riley. It was quite loud, quite deep and a bit croaky. Could it really have been Maia? The only sounds I had heard from her to that point were noisy yawns, blood curdling yelps and adorable little woofs while she was dreaming but never a full voice bark. The Forever Hounds Trust team said they had never heard her bark in kennels and she had been living with me for over six months and I hadn't heard her bark either. It must have been Maia.

On the one hand it was great that she was confident enough to use her voice, on the other this wasn't a habit I was keen to encourage. Luckily Maia only gives the odd 'woof' when she gets extremely over-excited while playing and it hasn't developed into an issue. It is a bit odd that she has such a deep bark though. The sound really doesn't fit with her elegant frame. It is yet another anomaly about that weird little lurcher.

There were other subtle signs that Maia was coming out of her shell. I went out on a walk and as usual grabbed some poo bags, treats, phone and keys. While I was walking round the field, I went to get a poo bag but found my pocket was empty. I knew I had put some in there. As I pushed my fingers to the bottom of my pocket, they kept on going straight through the bottom. Closer inspection revealed a not inconsiderable hole in the mesh lining of my pocket.

A few days later, I had exactly the same thing happen but this time I was wearing a different fleece. That was some coincidence. I didn't think for a second that Maia might be implicated. The following day it happened again but this time she had got careless and the penny finally dropped. As I picked my fleece up from where it had laid since our walk the day before, I heard something rustle. It didn't take long for me to find where it was coming from. There was another small hole in the lining of my pocket but this time I found the bag of treats left over from yesterday's walk pulled half way out through the hole. I knew Tam wouldn't dream of doing such a thing. There was only one other possible explanation. I now had holes in the pockets of three of my dog walking fleeces thanks to a greedy little lurcher who had found herself a free meal. I would never be able to leave treats in my pockets again!

It wasn't just me who had to keep my wits about me when Maia was around. Tam also found himself on the receiving end of her new found confidence. One afternoon they were dozing on the sofa. Well, Tam was dozing. Maia was working out what mischief she could get herself into. After much thought, she launched herself off the sofa, pounced on her toy, did a couple of spins, grabbed her toy and leapt back onto the sofa. Tam was rudely awoken and his peace was further disrupted when Maia flung her toy onto his back and proceeded to bite at it in a very grabby way. Tam looked mildly irritated but knew his slight annoyance wasn't enough to deter this pointy nosed little weirdo any more. Maia continued to grab at her toy and repeatedly threw it into the air. Each time it landed with a thud on Tam's back. He has the tolerance of a saint. Despite her very best efforts it became obvious that Tam wasn't going to join in. After a few more grabby bites, she settled on the sofa next to Tam with her toy still balanced on his back. She rested her head on him and fell asleep. By now Tam was quite resigned to being used as a pillow. He took it on the chin, shifted his weight a little and went back to sleep.

TWENTY-SIX - Month 7

Maia had now been living with us for seven months and I was starting to get a pretty good understanding about her personality, her likes and dislikes and her funny little ways. There was however one thing that continued to stump me. I had always wondered *what* Maia actually was - which breeds were in her genetic makeup. She had been described as a saluki cross but I wanted to be a bit more specific. After looking at several leading canine genetics companies I decided to invest in one that was considered reputable. They worked without photographs, all they required was a swab of DNA and they would test the sample in their lab, work their magic and notify me of her genetic makeup via an online account.

I waited with some anticipation for the DNA testing kit to arrive. Thankfully it came with clear step-by-step instructions. I had to get a sample of Maia's DNA by collecting some cheek cells using the swabs supplied. The instructions stated that I had to rub the swab against the inside of Maia's cheek for 30 seconds. I wasn't sure how she would react to me scrubbing away at the inside of her cheek but she coped really well, despite looking a little surprised. After double checking all the details, I packed it up in the envelope and sent it off.

I waited three long weeks before the results were confirmed. The suspense had been almost unbearable. With great anticipation I logged into my account to see Maia's test results. They came back as 75% greyhound which was what I had expected, 12.5% whippet, yes that made sense too, there is definitely whippet there, and 12.5% cocker spaniel. What the ...? COCKER SPANIEL?!! I have to admit I didn't see that one coming. I was quite taken aback. Maia didn't look or behave anything like a cocker spaniel.

The result was so unexpected I decided to email the DNA Company for an explanation. In their full and quite thorough reply they stuck to their guns and stated that all three breeds were detected at a high level of confidence. I'm still not sure I'm completely convinced about the cocker spaniel bit but it was certainly a fascinating, fun undertaking. I guess I'll never know exactly what Maia is. Like the events in her past some things will always remain a mystery.

Christmas was fast approaching and I wanted to get a nice Christmassy picture of Tam and Maia to put on the front of my business Christmas Cards. I try to do one every year and had always used Tam as my model. I am really not one for dressing up dogs but for my Christmas photo I make an exception. In previous years Tam had been a pretty fabulous Angel complete with halo and wings, he has done the 'fun in the snow whilst wearing tinsel' shot and a few years ago there was his crowning glory, Christmas tree. This year would be rather more of a challenge as I wanted to try and capture Tam and Maia together for my Christmas photo. I was expecting it to be a bit more tricky, but I never anticipated it would be quite as difficult as it was!

It was a simple idea, just Tam and Maia sitting next to each other wearing Santa hats. How hard could that be? I spent a few days gradually getting the dogs used to wearing their hats and although they didn't really see the point they both humoured me. Once they were happy wearing the hats, it was time to get 'the shot.'

I put Tam's hat on first but as he jumped up onto the sofa it slipped so I had to adjust it. Then Maia jumped on the sofa and straight off again, so Tam jumped off the sofa and his hat fell off. Round two. Tam on the sofa, then Maia on the sofa, Tam's hat on, Maia jumped

The 'x-rated' Christmas photo - edited version!

off the sofa. Urrgh! Considering that Maia spent most of her life on the sofa, it really didn't seem like I was asking too much for her to jump on the sofa and sit or lay still for 10 seconds! Round three. Tam on the sofa, hat on, Maia on the sofa, hat on, Maia starts investigating Tam's hat and nudges it down over his eyes. Straighten Tam's hat, Maia off the sofa, Maia's hat on the floor, Maia's hat in her mouth and now hurtling round the living room. Tam off the sofa joining in! Catch Maia, remove hat from mouth and wipe off slobber. Round four. Tam on sofa, hat on, Maia on the sofa, hat on, hold food treat just above the camera, frantically hit shutter button on camera and pray it takes. Did it take? Don't know. Tam and Maia both off the sofa and playing tug of war with Tam's hat! It was great to see them playing nicely together but really, their timing could have been better. I give up. This years' Christmas photo might just have to be photo of the dogs snuggling together with a Christmassy border round it.

OK, let's see what I got. I looked at the camera. Well, it had actually taken a shot and it wasn't half bad. Both dogs were sitting side by side, both wearing their hats, both almost looking at the camera. I reckon it would do. That was until I looked a little further down the photo and found that, thanks to Tam, it was X-rated! Oh well, with some strategic cropping I might just get away with it and nobody need ever know …

Being able to use the field became a real godsend, especially as the days were getting shorter and the weather was appalling. Unlike all the footpaths and bridleways, the field never became too muddy and it meant that the dogs could still have a good run every day. However, after weeks of unrelenting rain, the field flooded. A good third was underwater with two huge areas that looked like small lakes and a channel of flowing water that linked the two.

I took the dogs into the field and unclipped their leads. Their reactions when they saw the new water-feature couldn't have been more different. Tam was delighted and could hardly contain himself. It was like all his birthdays had come at once. Maia was horrified! She stood next to me looking up at me with a tragic look on her face. It was as if her whole world had fallen apart.

Tam immediately took off and ran straight through the middle of the first enormous lake. After circling round the top end of the field, he raced back down and launched himself back into the water. After much splashing around he eventually skidded to a halt, lay down in the centre and then plunged his whole face under. At first it was quite funny but after what seemed like ages, I started to wonder how long I should leave him before stepping in and reminding him that he had to come up for air! After a lot of underwater rooting Tam eventually resurfaced and, to his delight, he had managed to find a ball. Under all that water, it was quite an impressive feat.

Tam played around in the water for some time, dropping his ball, pouncing on it, grinding it into the mud under the water and then trying to find it again. As he dug excitedly at his ball with his front paws the previously clear water was starting to look decidedly murky. Tam was in his element.

After watching him for some time, Maia made a bold and somewhat surprising decision to launch herself into the water after him. With four huge leaps she had crossed the water and took off up the field with Tam in hot pursuit. They returned to the lake and with one final burst of over-confidence, Maia ran through the water and playfully nipped Tam on his bottom as she sped past. Did she really just do that? The audacity! Tam set off after her by which time Maia had realised her mistake. As soon as they both got to dry land Maia had a shakedown signalling the end of the game before Tam had a chance to retaliate. Sneaky!

Tam accepted it was game over and went back to digging his trench in the middle of the floodwater while Maia remained on dry land. That was the first and last time Maia ever nipped Tam. I don't think he realised what had happened at the time. Once her excitement died down, her respect for Tam quickly returned.

TWENTY-SEVEN - Month 8

Maia's rapidly escalating confidence was starting to show when she was around Tam. Up until this point, Tam had the luxury of being able to control Maia's actions with very little effort. There had been no overt aggression, not even the quietest grumble, but from day one his presence alone had been enough to command a level of respect from Maia. Unfortunately Maia was beginning to realise that despite being such a huge lump he was really just a big softy. She still had a healthy respect for him but she started to be less intimidated and his control over her movements started to slip.

This had been a hard barrier to break down as their relationship could never move forward as long as Maia remained wary of Tam. But times they were a changing and instead of getting worried and moving away from Tam, Maia was starting to - ever so gently and respectfully - push the boundaries.

Tam's tendency to lie in doorways had always been his preferred method to exert control over Maia and it had worked very well, but now Maia was rebelling. One afternoon Tam was lying apparently innocently in the kitchen but his position was blocking access to the back door. Up until now Maia would have just waited until he got out the way of his own accord or until I moved him, but control was shifting slightly in Maia's favour. Instead of waiting for me, Maia took matters into her own paws and in one easy leap, sprang right over the top of him and took herself out into the garden. The look on Tam's face was one of shock and bewilderment. It was priceless. How did she do that? Of course, after Maia had done it once and survived there was no stopping her. Tam's previously fail-safe method had lost its clout in that one single jump.

Tam wasn't just losing control over doorways. On another occasion he had positioned himself on the floor next to the sofa so that he was lying across Maia's take off point. The only way that Maia could get onto the sofa was to jump over him. Well, no-one keeps Maia from her sofa. She thought about it, considered her options then launched herself onto the sofa like a springbok. Poor Tam, he really didn't know how to respond and just resigned himself to the new normal.

For the first few months after her arrival Maia had been careful to give Tam a wide berth when their paths crossed in the cottage but things had changed there too. Tam was finding it harder to contain Maia. She was so narrow, so sleek, once her confidence had grown she started to realise that she didn't need much room to slide past him. Even doorways held no challenge for her now. The final insult to Tam's authority came when I was sitting on the sofa and he came over for some attention. As I was giving him a good scratch Maia went into the kitchen to have a drink. When she came back into the living room she spotted a tiny gap between Tam and me and without hesitation squeezed herself into it and parked herself between us. Fair play to Maia, that was another pretty bold move! Tam bless him, accepted it without a challenge. I gave them both a good scratch but this was something I would have to keep an eye on. I didn't want Tam to get resentful and feel he had to escalate his behaviour as his authority and control started to slip.

Maia wouldn't have dreamt of pushing past Tam before but after she had found that she could outsmart him once she started to do so with great regularity. I didn't tolerate Tam's door-blocking but as he was here first, he was entitled to certain privileges. Tam's position as 'top dog' might have taken a little bit of a knock but it wasn't enough to change the overall dynamic. Tam would always be the leader and Maia was definitely happy being the follower. Maybe, just maybe, Maia's increased confidence around Tam might *help* their relationship. If Maia was less intimidated by him she might be more motivated to play with him - perhaps even the rougher games that Tam loves. I was keeping everything crossed.

In order to keep things interesting I took a particularly tough teddy bear to the field for them to play with. It is a rope 'skeleton' so I felt it would be robust enough to stand up to the abuse it was about to receive. I knew that Tam would want to be at the front of the queue to play with it so Maia would have to wait patiently for her turn. You might think that taking two toys to the field would give them both something to play with but you can guarantee that whichever toy Maia had, Tam would want.

I threw the toy and Tam and Maia took off across the field in hot pursuit. Of course Maia left Tam standing and reached the toy way before him but she was going much too fast to grab it. As she circled, Tam had time to catch up and he grabbed the toy. This sent Maia into crazy zoomies mode and she sped round the field with Tam standing in the middle of the circle with the toy in his mouth looking bemused. He put the toy down for a second and Maia saw her opportunity and came in for a second attempt. Tam saw her coming just in time and grabbed the toy again but this time Maia was determined. She snatched the toy but Tam was ready for her and they both had a good-humoured tug-of war. Maia put up a brave fight Tam's bulk won out in the end. Maia accepted defeat and took off round the field again. It makes my heart sing every time I see her tearing around that field. Tam and Maia had really struggled to find a way to play together but now Maia was so much braver they were able to play in a way that couldn't have been possible just a few weeks before. This was a real turning point in their friendship. Finally they were working out how to play together and I couldn't have been more delighted!

Tam's idea of play ...

Maia's idea of play

TWENTY-EIGHT - Month 9

Maia's transformation was continuing unabated and she wanted to play more and more with Tam. On one of our daily visits to the field the dogs were both feeling playful. They really wanted to play chase but these games are always over before they have begun - until today. As I let the dogs off their leads they both ran up the field. After a quick sniff Maia took off in turbo mode and Tam decided to join her. In their eagerness they forgot to check who was doing the chasing and who was being chased. They took off in opposite directions and kept lapping each other but neither thought to change direction! It was great. Finally accidentally, they had found how to have a run together without Maia disappearing into the distance leaving Tam lagging behind. Tam had completed three large circles and Maia nearly six, but who's counting. They both had a great chase and looked very happy with the outcome.

It was late on Sunday evening and I noticed that Maia had a small discharge coming from one of her eyes. I was concerned as only one eye was affected which could mean that Maia had scratched her eye or got something in it. I cleaned it up and couldn't see anything obvious but eye injuries can be serious so I called my out of hours vet for advice. He felt it should be OK to wait until the next morning. Cue another sleepless night worrying about how Maia would cope at the vets.

When I woke the following morning I was greeted by quite a sight. Both of Maia's eyes were now very red and inflamed and there was thick gunge coming from both of them. It was almost certainly an infection. As it was a bank holiday, I had to drive to the vet's main hospital. Luckily, when we arrived it was very quiet and I was able to take the dogs straight in.

As before, Tam greeted the vet and then stood reassuringly close to Maia while she completely shut down. It was so sad to see as she had been doing so incredibly well, but this was an exceptional circumstance. The vet checked Maia's eyes and put in some dye to check that the surfaces weren't damaged. Luckily all was good. It was just had an eye infection and some eye drops would take care of it. Once we returned home Maia was none the worse except for having yellow dye stains running down her face. My challenge however was only just beginning. I had to get eye drops in her eyes twice a day for the next seven days starting from that evening. How hard could that be?

Administering eye drops can be a tricky process. You really need three hands to do it. One hand to steady the dog, one to hold open the eye and one to squirt the eye drops. I didn't have a helper so it was just going to be me versus Maia.

I prepared the tube of eye drops so it was ready to go, wedged Maia between my knees, opened her eye nice and wide, lined up the nozzle, squirted in the drops ... and missed. Round two. As before, I had Maia firmly yet gently gripped between my knees, eye drops at the ready, but now Maia was on to me. In my defence, the vet had it easy as Maia was so scared she froze. In that moment it would have been possible to do anything to her with no resistance. Now we were back home she was full of fight and made it clear that she wasn't going to make things easy. My second attempt was slightly more successful than the first as at least I hit the target, but rather annoyingly I didn't quite get enough drops out so it had to go to round three. At last, success! I managed to keep Maia still, got a good shot at the eye and Maia received the correct dose. We were half way there. Just one more eye to go. Unfortunately for me it was Maia's left eye. In order to get drops into the left eye, I would have to administer the correct dose with my left hand. As a right-hander, this could be a bit of a challenge.

As I started to fumble with the drops Maia sensed my incompetence and realised that she could easily get the upper hand. As before, I wedged her between my knees, opened her eye, but this time just as I squeezed the tube, she wriggled and the drops landed on her cheek. It was seriously annoying seeing the drops sitting there just a couple of millimetres off target. By this time Maia's patience was starting to wear thin. As I tried to keep hold of her she got more and more wriggly. With her lovely sleek coat, she was a slippery little blighter. Round 6. By this time we were both getting fed up so I decided that speed was of the essence. I would pin Maia - gently - to the sofa, aim and fire. It worked! The perfect shot. The drops landed right on target. I am not sure who was more relieved, Maia or me. Only another 12 hours and we would have to do it all over again. Luckily my skill levels increased significantly and by the end of the week we were both getting pretty good at it. I really struggle with forcibly doing anything unpleasant to animals even if I know it is for their own good. The experience was certainly more traumatic for me than for Maia. Luckily there was no long-term damage to our friendship. She quickly forgave me, and I am just grateful that Tam didn't catch the infection too!

Mutual bone chewing descends
into anarchy

TWENTY-NINE ~ Month 10

I had been looking forward to longer, lighter days and better weather so I could start to take Maia out and about a bit more. The opportunity to people-watch through the stock fence at the field had helped her get up close to numerous walkers and dogs and she was now happy to approach most people she met. I was hoping to take her out to some new places and start taking her round to our friends' homes.

Sadly our plans were abruptly halted with the outbreak of Covid-19. There's nothing like a global worldwide pandemic to thwart ones plans! On the upside, I could spend loads of time at home with the dogs catching up on all those little jobs I never had enough time to do. On the downside, the next stage of Maia's training would have to be put on hold.

Ever since Maia had triumphed over Tam's door blocking antics their relationship had blossomed. His constant need to remind her that he was in charge started to wain leaving him free to relax and to actually enjoy her company. It always takes a long time for Tam to change his behaviour. I can show him a better way but it is only once he has worked it out himself that he will make changes.

Tam and Maia were both lying side-by-side on the floor enjoying their usual morning bone chewing session. After a while Maia stopped chewing her bone and started to eye up Tam's. Despite having identical bones the dogs always think that the other one has got the better bone. They usually swap halfway through a chewing session but on this occasion Maia wanted to swap before Tam was ready. She waited reasonably patiently but Tam showed no signs of finishing so she took matters into her own paws. She still wasn't quite bold enough to take the bone from Tam so she reached across and started to sniff the bone that Tam was holding in his paws. Tam stopped chewing to see what Maia was up to and she seized her opportunity. The nerve of it! She started to chew Tam's bone *while he was still holding it!* The look on his face was a picture. Maia chewed on Tam's bone for another five minutes as he watched on in fascination and disbelief. Oh Tam, to think that your control over Maia had plummeted to this. To Maia it made perfect sense. She always struggled with how to hold a bone securely whilst chewing it. Now she had found the perfect solution!

It wasn't only Tam who was being taken advantage of. I noticed that Maia didn't seem to be drinking nearly as much as she usually did.

This was a concern as it wasn't 'normal' for her. I considered the possible reasons that could be causing her to drink less, such as diabetes, kidney disease, oral disease or urinary tract infections, but she wasn't showing any other symptoms. Her activity levels were the same so that couldn't explain it. She was happy and confident in her surroundings now so that couldn't be the reason. It was all a bit of a mystery. Then one day after our morning walk the reason became stomach-churningly clear.

Tam was always filthy when we got home from a walk and it would take all my attention to get him clean and dry. While I was busy washing and towel drying him, Maia had been going into the living room and helping herself to the water in my mug. I have no idea how long we had been sharing a drinking vessel but I know what Maia eats out on walks and I certainly wouldn't have been doing so by choice. I do have some sympathy for Maia as she shares a water bowl with Tam. Tam has slobbery jowls and even though I change their water twice a day, there is always a layer of slime at the bottom of it. Maia's disgust at sharing a water bowl with him was probably not dissimilar to my disgust at sharing a mug with her. I never left my drinks unattended after that.

As Maia was becoming so much more self-assured I felt that she was ready to play off-lead with her friends without the restriction of the longline. My only concern was that if she got too excited, she might try to bite the other dogs on the back of their necks, which is a typical behaviour for sighthounds. I didn't want Maia to accidentally hurt or frighten her friends during play, so I decided to be safe and teach her to accept wearing a muzzle. That way, even if she got too excited and went to bite, she would not cause injury.

Muzzle training should be an essential part of every dog's early training as most dogs will need to wear a muzzle at some stage of their life, such as when visiting the vet, to prevent scavenging on walks or to prevent biting and injuring others. Many dogs struggle with wearing a muzzle so I took things very slowly with Maia. I bought a lightweight greyhound muzzle that wasn't too bulky to make it as comfortable as possible. From her rather negative reaction when she saw it, it seemed likely she had worn one before! Instead of putting it straight on and securing the strap I wanted to give Maia time to get used to and accept it. If introduced carefully, she would learn that muzzles weren't really that bad and they could bring tasty rewards. As always, I broke her training down into tiny easily achievable steps and gave Maia the opportunity to have a really good look at the muzzle. She gave it a good sniff and during her inspection she briefly put her nose in. It was a lucky accident that I was quick to reward with praise and chicken.

It didn't take long for Maia to realize that good things happen when she puts her nose in the muzzle. Before long she was putting her nose in enthusiastically so I ended the session on a positive note.

In our next session Maia picked up where we had left off. I held up the muzzle and she trotted straight over and put her nose in. Great! The next step was for Maia to keep her nose in the muzzle for a little longer before getting her reward. I offered the treat through the muzzle but Maia got frustrated so I reverted back to plan A. Offer the muzzle to Maia, wait for her to put her nose in, wait for a second, take the muzzle away and reward. The next time I waited for a couple of seconds before removing the muzzle and gradually built up the time Maia had her nose in it before getting her reward. When she was happily putting her nose in I started doing up the strap, briefly at first, then gradually increasing the time she was wearing it. Maia enjoyed her muzzle training and it completely changed her attitude towards the muzzle from negative to positive.

Maia had been making such huge steps and many of her emotional scars were starting to heal. Around this time, I noticed a huge change in her physically. She had always held a lot of tension in her body and her muscles were always tight even when resting. As she had been so anxious for so long it was understandable that her body had become so set that way. Then when I was stroking Maia one evening I noticed that her muscles had started to relax. They were definitely softer, so I was able to give her a light massage.

Once Maia started to let go, the transformation was quite dramatic. Within the space of a couple of weeks she had completely let go of the tension she held in her shoulders and thighs and a few weeks later she even started releasing some of the tension in her back.

There were significant changes in Maia's behaviour that suggested she felt more comfortable now she had let go of all that tension. She started to lie on her back with her legs in the air like a proper greyhound! She also started to twist and contort her body into positions that weren't possible before as she was too tense. It was wonderful to see that now at last her body was healing too.

THIRTY - Month 11

The effects of the Covid lockdown were starting to bite. While I am sure that they were happy to have me at home all day to entertain them, Tam and Maia were getting bored. Just one walk a day instead of their usual two was taking its toll and Tam was struggling to understand why no one came over to stroke him in the field anymore. He started running along the fence line when people walked past, wagging his tail and barking to get them to notice him. He even threw in the odd play bow and had a mini-zoomies session to encourage them to play with him but they either stood back and admired him from a distance or just walked on by. Even Maia seemed disappointed that the walkers were keeping their distance. She followed them along the fence-line to the end of the field and then watched as they walked off into the distance. These were strange times indeed.

It is hard to believe that after nearly a year, Maia still surprised me with 'firsts'. Under Tam's tutorage, Maia was starting to play a bit rougher. She wasn't quite brave enough to go 12 rounds with him yet but she was happy to play rough with me. It is difficult to think

Extreme bravery

back to the tense, timid little hound that backed away if I looked at her and jumped at even the lightest touch. She couldn't be more different now. When Maia played rough I really had to have my wits about me as her reactions were lightning fast. She had perfected the karate chop so that she could string a whole line of them together like an unrelenting machine gun. I can take a few blows but when it gets too much, I bring in the big guns and let Tam take over. As long as Maia is excited enough, she is happy to pummel my substitute and Tam absolutely loves it.

Maia also loves it when I fling a throw over her head so she can't see anything and then push her around and rub her vigorously with the rest of the throw. I frequently stop to check that she is still enjoying herself - although I have no doubt that she would be quick to let me know if she wasn't! I lift the edge of the throw up with some trepidation to uncover a crazy face with a slightly manic eye looking up at me, ears folded inside out and teeth flashing. She usually puts her head back under the throw again to encourage me to carry on. These are the games that used to be reserved for Tam, but not anymore!

She also started to really enjoy tug of war games with her long-suffering chicken soft toy as her victim. She was surprisingly strong and *highly* competitive. When Maia played she definitely played to win. If I wanted to get the better of her I had to time it carefully and snatch the toy from her the moment she altered her grip. The only problem was that Maia was so fast that my reactions weren't quick enough to beat her fair and square. I usually either gave up before she did as I couldn't bear the sound of the toy tearing under the strain, or I'd ask her to drop her toy mid-game. It was a bit mean but I had to win sometimes! When Maia was particularly excited, she even started to play tug-of-war with Tam which was a very bold move on her part. It was so funny seeing her pulling with all her might to get the toy from Tam while he stood barely making any effort at all. He always did just enough to make sure that Maia couldn't get the toy. Their tug of war always ended amicably. Tam would settle with the toy and have a doze, while Maia would have a shakedown and then go and find herself another toy to play with.

It was not all high energy games for Maia. Oh no. In between her playful outbursts she was still her usual lazy self. The weather had been really fantastic so we took advantage of the glorious sunshine and spent a bit more time in the evenings at the field. Did Maia use that time to do loads of extra running and sniffing? No chance. She ran half way across the field before flopping down onto the grass. She rolled onto her side lying flat out, closed her eyes and fell asleep. She would have stayed like that all evening if it weren't for some serious 'encouragement' from me. She is a complete sun-worshipper. She doesn't like it when it is too hot, but when the temperature hovers around the 20° Celsius mark, it's perfect.

On days when the weather was a bit overcast or a little cooler, Maia liked to join Tam as he patrolled the field. He used to get frustrated when she followed him around but he had got much more relaxed about it. He became resigned to the fact that Maia with her upbeat, positive attitude would be following him regardless so he just got on with it. Luckily for Tam, mother nature intervened and gave him the perfect opportunity to do some serious exploring without his cling-on following him every step of the way - stinging nettles!

The field was surrounded by a grassy bank that contained dozens of rabbit warrens. Luckily for Tam - and the rabbits - they were all thickly shrouded with nettles. Tam's coat was so thick he could bulldoze his way through a forest of nettles and wouldn't feel a thing. He emerged from the other side with an incredible collection of bugs and spiders stuck in his coat that had been happily minding their own business before he came along. Maia and her ridiculously thin coat and paper-thin skin knew just how painful nettles could be and didn't attempt to follow him. They gave Tam an unrivalled opportunity to explore every rabbit hole in peace and he took full advantage of it. As he climbed up the bank he left Maia standing at the bottom looking longingly after him. I'm with Tam on this one. He has put up with so much over that past 11 months, he has earned some alone time. After completing his investigations Tam returned to the grassy field and got a lovely pokey welcome from Maia. These two were definitely striking up a genuine friendship. These little moments of affection were truly heart-warming to see.

There is a big field close to home with a footpath through it. For most of the year it has sheep and horses grazing so dogs have to be kept on leads but for a few months in late spring, the livestock is removed and the field is left to grow hay. This provides a lovely opportunity to let the dogs off-lead and have a good run.

Over the winter months Maia had become quite friendly with a few of the dogs we met on our walks but she never had the opportunity to have a proper sprinty game with them as she was always on the long-line. Now the field was empty, we could meet up with her friends and let them off so they could really enjoy themselves.

There were a couple of dogs in particular who were friendly high energy speed merchants, and Maia always got really excited watching them play. Now it was finally time to let her join in.

I waited until the dogs had calmed after their initial excitement at meeting each other, then I unclipped Maia's lead and she was off! I never dared dream that one day she would be able to run free with her friends in a public space yet here she was living her best life. As they raced away they proved to be very evenly matched. Maia would win hands down in a race on the straight but she wasn't so good at cornering so the other dogs were able to make up some ground. They ran around at breakneck speed for several minutes before taking time out to catch their breath. It had been a very long time since Maia had been able to have a proper sprinty game with evenly matched opponents.

Although she was very friendly and respectful to the other dogs she still had to learn how to play nicely with them. I was concerned that in her excitement she might try to nip the other dogs so I had her muzzle at the ready just in case she needed it. It wasn't long before they were off again. While they were running Maia closed in to nip one of the other dogs. As she did, the other dog sensed what she was doing and immediately stopped and ended the game. They couldn't have made it any clearer than that! Maia stopped too then there was a slightly uneasy standoff as Maia's friends gave her time to understand the message. Once she was calm, they took off again.

It was fascinating to watch the dogs teaching Maia *how* to play. They were so patient and tolerant with her. Maia only made that error twice before she learnt that important rule of play and she hasn't made that mistake since. I can now just let her off-lead to play with her friends, relax and enjoy the spectacle.

Back at home and Tam was so much more relaxed around Maia now and his mood had really mellowed. He started to stand by the sofa with his tail wagging and gave a super quiet 'woof' to try and engage Maia in play. Sadly, more often than not Maia snubbed him but Tam was definitely making many more playful approaches to her. He finally seemed to be extending a genuine paw of friendship to Maia with no mistrusting undertones.

Tam still struggled with the snuggling thing. We were enjoying a lovely peaceful evening, Maia was lying flat on her side, fast asleep on the duvet when Tam went and lay down next to her. He was clearly trying very hard to connect with her so he rolled onto his side and rested his huge head right on top of Maia's little skinny face. Oh Tam, that was a lovely gesture but Maia really didn't look very comfortable. It was still unusual for Tam to initiate snuggles. He tried so hard but he still didn't quite understand the effect his attempts at snuggling had on Maia. In this latest effort, not only was he crushing her face but he was also partially smothering her too. After a little readjustment that at least enabled Maia to breathe they fell asleep cheek to cheek. It had only taken about 10 months longer than anticipated, but it was definitely worth the wait.

Still learning how to snuggle

THIRTY-ONE ~ Month 12

How time has flown. It is almost impossible to believe it has been a whole year since Maia turned our lives upside down. My life has changed considerably. I now feel twice as guilty whenever I have to go out and leave the dogs home alone for any length of time. I now have to tell two pairs of sad eyes that I 'will be back in a minute' knowing full well that a minute was going to be four hours.

When I return home, I can no longer make myself a nice cup of tea, sit down on the sofa, relax and watch a bit of television. No, I come home, walk the dogs, get home, give Tam some 1-2-1 attention, give Maia some 1-2-1 attention, make their dinner, watch them eating to make sure that Maia doesn't help herself to Tam's food, then spend what's left of the evening sitting on the floor as the dogs have already hogged the sofa!

I am twice as poor as in my pre-Maia days. The hope of Maia being slightly less expensive than Tam has fallen short of expectations. Far from being a low maintenance lurcher, Maia has proved to be almost as expensive to keep as Tam. She now has a wardrobe worth substantially more than my own: two new polar-neck coats, one polar neck jumper, a rain coat, and a super-warm coat. Number of new tops I've bought for myself over the past twelve months = 1.

My social life has gone down the pan. It is now limited to meeting up with friends for a quick socially distanced coffee. Gone are weekends away in Dorset and day trips to locations around the UK. I can barely remember nights out at the theatre, dinner parties and big family get-togethers.

I have given up on ever having a clean and tidy home and garden. Despite my best efforts no sooner have I cleaned the house, my two yobbos quickly return it to the state it was in prior to hours of elbow grease. Muddy paw-prints decorate the newly vacuumed carpets and toys get strewn all over the floor within seconds of returning the last toy to the toy box. Within minutes, the cottage looks just as it did before I spent all day cleaning it. All I have to show for my efforts are sore joints, broken nails and aching back.

As for the garden, my nice green lawn now resembles Glastonbury after a particularly wet festival. All the little plants that I nurtured over the years have been completely flattened after finding themselves lining the route of the zoomies circuit. Even well-established shrubs have received a good thrashing by becoming crash barriers.

I really miss going hands-free on the long walks up on the hills. Having one dog on a longline makes it so much harder to relax, 'just be' and enjoy the beautiful scenery and amazing wildlife. The alternative - having Maia off lead - would probably lead to a some-what more stressful walk ... and considerably less wildlife!

So yes, my life has changed beyond recognition since Maia arrived but I don't regret a thing. I have been more than repaid for my sacrifices by the joy, the laughs and the love that I have received from that pointy nosed little weirdo and the happy look on Tam's face when Maia reciprocates his friendly advances.

It can be challenging taking on a rescue dog. Many have issues to a greater or lesser degree. Maia was an extreme case, but it is hugely rewarding knowing that just 12 months ago she was living in a kennel, terribly fearful of humans, completely shut down, yet now as I write this, she is stretched out in her favourite spot on the sofa, poking me in my back with her claws to get my attention. She has now rolled on to her back and is exposing her hairless tummy with her legs in the air and a silly toothy grin on her face. Yep, that did it. I can't resist that look. Excuse me for a minute I just need to give Madam some attention ...

Where was I? Oh yes. Moments before I was so rudely interrupted, Maia had just finished having a good Karate choppy game with Tam (yes he does still have both eyes intact) and she has a belly full of hypoallergenic, grain-free hugely expensive food. Her duvet is in the washing machine, her coats are drying and her minion has just brought her toys in from the garden as it was beginning to rain.

Tam is lying at my feet, deep in REM sleep, his muzzle, eyes, tail and paws twitching. I used to think that when he slept, he dreamt of chasing squirrels and rabbits across the field. I now think that he is dreaming about avoiding Maia's blows!

So who is Maia? When I first saw her trembling with fear at the back of her kennel, I remember thinking how much I wanted to find out *who* she really was. Behind the stress and anxiety, behind the evasive behaviour I knew there was so much more to this little lurcher. She was so shut down when she arrived, but as her confidence grew her personality began to shine through. She has such a happy and upbeat attitude which is incredible considering all that she has been through. Her zest for life is inspirational and her positivity is contagious. It is hard to feel down when Maia is bouncing and spinning with excitement just because I suggested we go into the kitchen! There is just one thing that makes Maia's mood falter - RAIN! Even the lightest shower. Sad background music and an emotive voiceover and she would make the perfect visual for a tragic appeal.

Maia is soooo lazy. She spends much of her day asleep on the sofa but when she is awake she is wide awake and gives everything 100%. She is extremely playful with a funny, cheeky personality that makes me laugh out loud many times every day. She is an absolute joy to live with.

When I think back to how fearful she was when she arrived it was impossible to imagine that she could ever become so incredibly nosey but now she is the first into *everything*! Nothing is safe from a thorough pointy nosed investigation. It's a far cry from her early melt-downs at the merest rustle of a plastic bag. She *loves* food and her appetite seems insatiable, which has helped no end with her training. Food is power! Maia really loves to learn and always tries to please. Even if she does do something I would rather she didn't - like decapitating my flowers - she has a really sweet innocent 'who, me?' look on her face which of course enables her to get away with pretty much anything!

Maia is incredibly sensitive which isn't surprising considering her history and I still have to watch her carefully when we are out and about. She is very expressive and signals her emotions clearly, so I can always see if she is coping well or if she needs a bit of extra support. Maia has an incredibly high sense of self-preservation. I can only imagine that she must have felt pain in the past to cause her to fear it to such an extreme now. She does have a tendency to over-react such as the dis-proportionate volume of the yelp elicited after she brushed past me in a poorly judged zoomies moment!

The last aspect of Maia's personality that I find truly overwhelming is her incredible capacity to love. She is not a cuddly dog but loves to snuggle next to me, resting her head on my arm and staring up into my eyes with a look in her eyes that is absolutely priceless.

So, who is Maia? Far from being a nervy shrinking violet, she is a wonderfully happy, sweet, gentle, sensitive, cheeky, cocky Diva with bags of personality with a limitless amount of love to give. I am sure that her personality will continue to develop and she will reveal even more about who she is as she continues her rehab.

Tam and Maia have had quite a roller coaster journey and it took them longer to work things out than I ever anticipated. Even in the past few weeks they have been making new positive steps and I am confident their relationship will get stronger and stronger as time goes on. As things stand, Tam seems to be the one making the most effort. He frequently approaches Maia and gives her a comforting friendly sniff and he has learnt to moderate his behaviour around her. After polite introductions he does a lovely play bow and a half volume 'woof' to encourage her to play which is occasionally reciprocated. You can't knock the fella for trying.

They do have wonderful moments where they rub faces affection-ately in a gentle loving manner and on those rare occasions when they are both feeling playful at the same time they can even enjoy some good games. They might not spend every moment snuggled together but they are definitely very fond of each other.

Maia remains respectful of Tam but she is no longer afraid of him. She takes such liberties around him but he totally accepts it. She still has a pretty sketchy understanding of personal space which used to be an issue for Tam, but now he has accepted that is just part of who she is. He almost seems amused by a lot of Maia's

'That' look

antics and seems to genuinely enjoy having her around. He has even learnt that being poked in the face is a sign of affection!

Maia has proved that time and love really can conquer all. It was a huge commitment taking in such a troubled hound and she has dominated my life for the last year. I have had to consider Maia in everything I have done and continue to do so, but I never forget that a troubled dog is seldom born that way. Maia is just a reflection of the challenges she faced in her early years. Every dog has the right to a happy fear-free life and it is my responsibility to ensure that Maia has the life she deserves.

She has reaffirmed to me how important it is to see the world from the animal's perspective and epitomises why I am so motivated to give animals a voice. We humans are the clever ones. It is up to us to see the world from our dogs' perspective and do everything we can to give them their best life. After all, we chose to bring them into our lives so it is our responsibility to make sure that we make decisions and choices that they would make if they were able.

So what's next for Maia? She has already come such a long way on her journey and is barely recognisable from the scared hound she once was. She has come on further than I could ever have hoped for but we still have a few things to work on. In the home she is really just like a normal dog. I don't have to modify my behaviour around her at all now. I can step over her, drop things next to her and even flap big black bin bags in front of her and she doesn't bat an eyelid. She is now happy to approach people she doesn't know when we are out and will calmly wait with us as we natter but she still gets uncomfortable if they try to look at her or touch her. I still watch her closely during interactions as her response can be very subtle - just a quick look away or a little step back - but she knows that I am ready to help her if she needs it. Similarly, she is happy for visitors to sit next to her in the cottage, but if they try to engage her it is a bit too much. She may never be completely happy with strangers approaching and interacting with her but I feel there is a definite possibility she will improve as time goes on. It has after all still only been twelve months and she has held on to these fears for years.

Maia is ready to see more of the world. I hope to get her out so she can visit new areas and meet new people but as always, I will be guided entirely by Maia. I still have the dream of watching her run free in the beautiful open countryside that surrounds my home. Her confidence has grown to the point that she doesn't panic and bolt if she sees anyone approaching, her recall is excellent and she doesn't seem worried by other dogs any more. When she arrived it seemed like a delusion to ever hope that Maia might one day enjoy the same freedom as Tam but now I am hopeful that one day we might reach that goal. If there is one thing Maia has taught me, it's to never underestimate her.

In my final reflections I must pay tribute to Tam. The kindest, most generous, most tolerant dog I could ever have wished for to accompany me on this journey. The things he has experienced and the challenges he has faced over the past twelve months cannot be underestimated. He has gone from doting new brother, through the unease and communication challenges that impacted their early relationship, to long-suffering big brother and now, best friend. I do not know many dogs that would tolerate as much as he has. I could never have helped Maia so much without him. I provided the framework for Maia to learn and Tam filled in the gaps. That's not to say that he didn't have his down days, but his generosity was never in doubt. Thank you with all my heart Tam.

So, as our first year together comes to an end I can look back with joy, satisfaction and an overwhelming sense of pride. Maia couldn't be happier and Tam has at last got the friend and companion that I had always hoped for him. I look forward with a completely open heart to see what the future holds for Tam, Maia and me. Maia has so much more to give, so much more growing to do. I feel that in another twelve months she will be barely recognisable from the hound she is today. I am so excited to be a part of her future, to see her grow and develop. Heaven help us!

A little post-note

I am delighted to report that nearly 14 months after Maia came to join us my dream of her seeing her run free was finally realised. We went for a walk up onto the downs and I unclipped her lead and let her run with Tam in thousands of acres of open countryside.

Whenever I whistled she raced back to me and her face was a picture. I honestly can't tell you how it made me feel seeing her running and exploring with Tam. Proof that dreams really can come true.

Home ... forever

Forever Hounds Trust

If you feel you might be able to offer a wonderful home to a hound in need there is no better place to start than Forever Hounds Trust.

Forever Hounds Trust is a registered charity (number 1131399), originally established in 1996 under the name Greyhound Rescue West of England. The name was changed to Forever Hounds Trust in 2016. It was originally set up in the West of England to rescue, rehabilitate and rehome greyhounds and lurchers but they now have regions of operations and kennels from which to care for and address the welfare issues of these dogs, across England. They also rescue dogs from Ireland, where conditions can be particularly cruel for sighthounds, and they were even involved in the rescue and of greyhounds from China when the notorious Macau racing track closed in 2018.

Manned by a small team of dedicated staff and an army of wonderful volunteers, Forever Hounds Trust is a really amazing charity. They have rehomed over 10,000 unwanted, abandoned or abused greyhounds and lurchers (a sighthound crossed with any other breed) and remain absolutely committed to helping as many hounds in need as possible. Their mission is to rescue and care for unwanted abused or abandoned greyhounds, to find safe, loving permanent homes for them, to care for all their hounds using best practice and to strive for and promote improved welfare for all sighthounds.

Sighthounds and lurchers really are the most amazing dogs. They might not have the cute fluffy exterior of some other breeds but these sensitive, gentle loving dogs really do make the most amazing pets. Contrary to popular belief, greyhounds are actually quite lazy and don't require a huge amount of exercise - Maia being a typical example! Depending on what they are crossed with, some lurchers have higher energy levels but there really is a sighthound suitable for every home. Forever Hounds Trust are committed to matching the right hound with the right home, and their experience means that dogs are rarely returned. New families receive support and advice from professional behaviourists for the dog's entire life.

If you think you may be able to offer a rescued hound a forever home please take a look at the charity's website: **www.foreverhoundstrust.org.** You will find all that you need to know about how to offer a fabulous sighthound a home along with loads of really helpful information about how to look after and care for your hound. You could also check out the Forever Hounds Trust Facebook page (**www.facebook.com/ForeverHoundsTrust)**, where my own amazing journey with Maia began. There is loads of news about what the charity has been up to, wonderful examples of hounds who have gone on to find their forever homes and of course details of hounds who are still looking for their own comfy sofa.

As Forever Hounds Trust is a registered charity, they rely entirely on donations to continue their wonderful work. There are many ways that you can donate to help support their work helping hounds in need. Please go to the website to find out how to donate. All gifts go directly towards the welfare of the hounds by providing essential veterinary care, food, kennel fees and transport costs.

Volunteers are the lifeblood of Forever Hounds Trust and they are always looking for passionate people to join their volunteer family. Volunteering opportunities are almost endless so wherever you live, however much time you have and whatever your skillset you can help make a real difference. If you want to meet friendly, like-minded people with a real passion for helping hounds please go to the website where you can apply to be a Forever Hounds Trust volunteer.

Thank you for caring.

FOREVER HOUNDS TRUST

Matching greyhounds and lurchers to happy homes

A little bit about Healing

Healing is a natural holistic energy therapy where Healing Practitioners link with natural energy that surrounds us and then send it to the recipient to bring benefit on physical, emotional and spiritual levels.

Promoting Healing as a Natural and Holistic Choice for All

We all have energy flowing round our bodies. Sometimes through stress, injury or disease our energy levels become depleted and the flow of energy becomes blocked. Healing helps by clearing the energy blockages, replenishing our energy levels and jump-starting our own body's natural healing processes to bring about deep self-healing.

This wonderful, gentle therapy has many benefits. Clients often report that healing eases physical and emotional pain, reduces stress, lifts mood, increases energy and instils a sense of peace and calm. It is really relaxing and can be given without any direct physical contact so can be invaluable when working with extremely fearful animals like Maia. Healing also enables a profound line of communication to open between animal and practitioner, breaking down psychological and emotional barriers and quickly builds trust and confidence. Without healing, I have no doubt that Maia's rehab would have taken much, much longer.

Healing is non-denominational so no faith or religious beliefs are necessary to give healing or receive benefit and most people can learn how to send healing energy. It is a complementary therapy with no unpleasant side effects and works really well alongside conventional medicine.

Healing is a wonderful therapy, but it is not an alternative to traditional veterinary medicine. If you have an animal that you feel may benefit from healing, you must always take them to a conventional vet for diagnosis and treatment advice before seeking assistance from a healing practitioner.

If you want to learn more about healing, The Healing Trust is a good place to start. It is the largest professional UK based healing organisation. Founded in 1954 it is a charity that promotes health and well-being through healing and has a great program for training Healing Practitioners.

For more information about healing or to find a Healing Practitioner near you, go to www.thehealingtrust.org.uk.

How to find a Canine Behaviourist

Dogs commonly develop unwanted behaviours at some stage in their lifetime. Unfortunately, many behaviours that humans consider undesirable are naturally occurring behaviours that make perfect sense to our dogs. For example, if a dog is fearful of people, they might bark and lunge at passers-by to dissuade them from approaching. It can be a very effective strategy, but it's not usually considered desirable by the owner hanging on to the other end of the lead! Or a dog left home alone might get bored, lonely or anxious, so they start destroying the soft furnishings to help them cope with their stress and frustration. It may seem that they are being deliberately naughty, but many unwanted behaviours are driven by fear, anxiety, frustration or confusion, and our dogs are just behaving the best way they know how at the time. In many ways they are simply communicating to us that that they are struggling and that they need a bit of help.

Commonly reported problems include aggression, nervousness, destructive behaviours, excessive barking, separation issues and inappropriate toileting. These unwanted behaviours can be incredibly stressful for both dog and owner and can compromise their quality of life. Despite the difficulties, many owners learn to live with these issues but with a little understanding, time and commitment, a lot can be done to resolve them.

If you are having any issues with your own dog's behaviour it is essential that you first take them to your vet to rule out any underlying medical conditions that might be contributing. Many problem behaviours have a medical cause such as undiagnosed pain, so it is vital to address health issues before trying to modify the behaviour.

Once your dog has been given a clean bill of health, you might find it helpful to seek the services of a canine behaviour specialist. A behaviourist will discuss all aspects of your dog's life in order to gain a complete picture of the issues and the reasons behind them. They will discuss your dog's daily routine, home environment, diet, medical history and the relationship they have with all family members as well as looking at the problem behaviours in detail. They will design a behaviour plan tailored to your dog's individual needs and support you as you work through the issues.

It can be quite bewildering trying to find the right person to help you with your dog, so here are a few things to look out for:-

- Look for someone who is registered with the ABTC (Animal Behaviour and Training Council) such as members of the APBC (Association of Pet Behaviour Counsellors) or similar organisations.

- Members of these professional organisations have all attained a high level of academic achievement and practical competence. They are also fully insured and follow a strict code of conduct.

- They all work on vet referral.

- They all attend regular ongoing training to ensure they have the most relevant, up-to-date knowledge of the latest most effective techniques.

- They all use high-welfare, reward-based approaches and avoid using any equipment that causes pain or instils fear in your dog.

- Trust your instincts. If you don't feel comfortable with the approach they are using, find another behaviourist.

It can be challenging changing long-held and well-established behaviours in our pets. It's hard enough changing our own behaviour and we know why we are doing it! However, a suitably qualified and experienced behaviourist should be able to help you address the problem behaviour and then help rebuild the trust and relationship you have with your dog. It might take a lot of work, but it is well worth the effort in the long run.

Lisa Benn is an Animal Behaviourist and Healing Practitioner with over twenty years' experience working with troubled animals. Always fascinated by human and animal behaviour she attained a BSc (Hons) in Psychology in 2000. After many years working with horses she then specialised in canine behaviour and was awarded an MSc in Companion Animal Behaviour Counselling in 2013. Lisa is accredited to the Healing Trust and has been mentoring and training students in animal healing since 2010.

Lisa established her animal behaviour and healing practice 'Understanding Pets' in 2002. Her empathic animal-centred approach combines an extensive knowledge of animal behaviour with intuitive healing. She is passionate about strengthening the relationship people have with their animals through building confidence and trust, increasing awareness and mutual under-standing.